SONNET

"In this daring new translation of ⸺ unique blend of scholarship and tender ⸺ sophistication. 'A breath about nothing. A blowing in god. A wind.' (I.3) The sonnets themselves are famously obscure, and this new translation does not try to expose that which was meant to be hidden or domesticate the difficult. 'Hardly anyone helped the earliest riskers' (II.24), as Burrows renders these lines, and in so doing brings his readers into the original risk of Rilke's voice anew—fresh and strange—for readers today. We hear the original song in these resonant translations, with music that reaches in and makes new music within the reader."

PÁDRAIG Ó TUAMA, POET, PEACE ACTIVIST, AND HOST
OF "POETRY UNBOUND"

"Mark S. Burrows' elegant and exacting translation of Rainer Maria Rilke's *Sonnets to Orpheus* offers readers what I had long thought impossible to find: a faithful and musical rendering of one of the most important poetic sequences of the last century. Add to that his compelling versions of Rilke's Eighth and Ninth *Duino Elegies*, which were composed in the same glorious month as the *Sonnets to Orpheus*, and you have Rilke's final words on desire, creativity, and the spiritual life: 'Isn't the secret ruse / of this reticent earth, when it urges lovers on, / that each and everything delights in their feeling?' Yes, yes, yes!"

CHRISTOPHER MERRILL, DIRECTOR OF THE INTERNATIONAL WRITING
PROGRAM (IOWA) AND AUTHOR OF *ON THE ROAD TO LVIV*

"Mark S. Burrows displays a double fidelity to Rilke's poetic genius and inimitable mystical depth in this remarkable rendition of the Sonnets. His deft attention to the secret music of Orpheus has created a gem of auditory imagination."

RICHARD KEARNEY, AUTHOR OF *POETICS OF IMAGINING*
AND *THE NOVEL SALVAGE*

"This is the translation of Rilke's *Sonnets to Orpheus* I have been waiting for. Finally, the poetry sings in English through the many finely tuned phrases and nuanced lines of another poet. That said, Mark S. Burrows is not afraid to let the unaccommodated strangeness of the original German darkly shine through his translations: those moments where Rilke pushes his language to the limit are captured in all their 'radiant obscurity.' No difficulties are easily resolved here, as so often in other translations, and the reader is thus allowed to read her way to a response and to be shaped in the precious moment of her uncertainty. I find myself at the threshold of the invisible, and alive, in these versions of *The Sonnets to Orpheus*, to the mystery."

EDWARD CLARKE, PROFESSOR OF ENGLISH, OXFORD UNIVERSITY, AND
AUTHOR OF *A BOOK OF PSALMS* AND *THE SECRET MIND OF ART*

"This new translation of Rilke's *Sonnets to Orpheus* comes to us at the most urgent of times, when, more than ever, the dehumanized and violent in our societies 'wants now to be praised.' In these beautiful, daring translations, Burrows returns to us the power and mystery of Rilke's original—the 'unknowing' qualities that drive his verse. And in Burrows' rendering, the *Sonnets to Orpheus* become for us guide and warning: a deep source to draw on as we face the shadow of our own spiritual and physical destruction."

ELLEN HINSEY, POET AND AUTHOR, MOST RECENTLY,
OF *THE INVISIBLE FUGUE*

"In this exceptionally sensual, boldly fresh translation of Rilke's famed *Sonnets to Orpheus*, we hear what Burrows describes as 'a voice resonant with a hope that does not look away from life.' As a poet, Burrows shows himself to be truly the translator Rilke readers in English have long been waiting for. My own understanding of Rilke—and of myself—deepened with every phrase. His beautiful Introduction and Afterword invite us to perceive, and receive, the gifts that Rilke is offering to Orpheus, yes, but also to each of us as readers."

STEPHANIE DOWRICK, AUTHOR OF *IN THE COMPANY OF
RILKE* AND *YOUR NAME IS NOT ANXIOUS*

"'Our life goes forth with transformation': this phrase is the watchword for Mark Burrows' fresh translation of Rilke's great poetic cycle, the *Sonnets to Orpheus*. With remarkable precision, Burrows renders the sense and feel of the original, its urgent language and shape-shifting metaphors. He brings to life again Rilke's endeavor to show how poetry is a way of living more fully the complexities and questions of our time on earth. In the revealing Introduction and Afterword that accompany the poems, he suggests how these sonnets seize us with language before we understand them, reminding us of Rilke's remarkable—and ceaseless to the point of obsessive—revisiting of the theme of transformation and the presence of now."

HILARY DAVIES, POET, ESSAYIST, AND LITERARY CRITIC, AND AUTHOR OF *EXILE AND THE KINGDOM*

"Everyone gives up on love, like poetry, and has to be reminded of its power and promise. This new translation of Rilke is such a reminding. Burrows translates what can't be translated: the English alembic for Rilke's Germanic soul. His rendering travels through and finally beyond language, not simply to negation, but to the heart of objects themselves."

BRADFORD MANDERFIELD, PROFESSOR OF THEOLOGY AT THE ATHENAEUM OF OHIO

SONNETS

TO

ORPHEUS

RAINER MARIA RILKE

✳ ✳✳

BILINGUAL EDITION

A NEW TRANSLATION
WITH AN INTRODUCTION AND AFTERWORD BY

MARK S. BURROWS

Monkfish Book Publishing Company
Rhinebeck, New York

Paperback ISBN 978-1-958972-39-7
eBook ISBN 978-1-958972-40-3

Library of Congress Cataloging-in-Publication Data

Names: Rilke, Rainer Maria, 1875-1926, author. | Burrows, Mark S., 1955-
    translator, writer of introduction, writer of afterword. | Rilke, Rainer
    Maria, 1875-1926. Sonette an Orpheus. | Rilke, Rainer Maria, 1875-1926.
    Sonette an Orpheus. English.
Title: Sonnets to Orpheus : a new translation / Rainer Maria Rilke ;
    translated into English with an introduction and afterword by Mark S.
    Burrows.
Description: Bilingual edition. | Rhinebeck, New York : Monkfish Book
    Publishing Company, 2024. | Includes bibliographical references. |
    Parallel text in German and English.
Identifiers: LCCN 2023051248 (print) | LCCN 2023051249 (ebook) | ISBN
    9781958972397 (paperback) | ISBN 9781958972403 (ebook)
Subjects: LCSH: Orpheus (Greek mythological character)--Poetry. | LCGFT:
    Poetry.
Classification: LCC PT2635.I65 S613 2024 (print) | LCC PT2635.I65 (ebook)
    | DDC 831/.912--dc23/eng/20231124
LC record available at https://lccn.loc.gov/2023051248
LC ebook record available at https://lccn.loc.gov/2023051249

Cover painting by Youqing Wang / wangfineart.com
Book and cover design by Colin Rolfe

Monkfish Book Publishing Company
22 East Market Street, Suite 304
Rhinebeck, New York 12572
(845) 876-4861
monkfishpublishing.com

For all who long to know that
"where words once were, discoveries now flow"
and dare to "dance the orange"

Sonnets to Orpheus I.15

CONTENTS

Introduction   xi

SONNETS TO ORPHEUS

First Part   3

Second Part   57

DUINO ELEGIES

The Eighth Elegy   118

The Ninth Elegy   124

Afterword: *"We Make the World Our Own"*   131

Acknowledgments   147

Notes for the Sonnets   151

Endnotes   159

About the Author   165

INTRODUCTION

The Sonnets to Orpheus were born of astonishment on the part of their author, Rainer Maria Rilke (1875–1926). They came to him unexpectedly during a three-week period in February of 1922, arousing the interest of readers across Europe when they were published in March of the following year. Indeed, the Austrian poet Hugo von Hofmannsthal wrote to Rilke to express his appreciation for these sonnets, extolling how these sonnets "set a new boundary-line for the realm of what can hardly be said"; he went on to say that he "found [himself] enchanted by the beauty and assuredness with which a subtle thought finds expression [in them], as with the admirable brushstroke of a Chinese painter: wisdom and rhythmic ornamentation in one."[1] In a letter written a year before his untimely death, Rilke suggested that the *Sonnets*—as with the *Elegies*, completed in the same month—reveal our work as "transformers of the Earth, [and] our entire existence, the flights and falls of our love, everything prepares us for this task."[2] The *Sonnets*, he went on to suggest, voiced the "particularities" of this work.

This collection arrived in stages as he was preparing to finish the *Duino Elegies*, begun a decade earlier but abandoned under the pressure of the war and the long period of depression that followed. By the summer of 1921, however, he felt he had regained a needed sense of composure and had finally found a place conducive to his hopes of completing that work: an austere medieval manor-house referred to as Château de Muzot, a stone tower nestled among the hills of the Rhone valley in the Swiss canton of Valais. Its seclusion provided the uninterrupted quiet Rilke had long sought for this project.

Within days of settling in he wrote to his mother of "the particular charm of Muzot," which had to do with its being "situated all alone in this impressive landscape, without a single nearby neighbor."[3] Though "wonderful and picturesque in its own way, it was not an easy place to live," he went on to say, but offered him a measure of the solitude he had lacked during the preceding years marked by short-term stays with friends and residencies in hotels funded by benefactors. Rilke's residence in this small "château," from the summer of 1921 until his death on December 29, 1926, became his longest continuous domicile since his childhood in Prague.

The first twenty-six sonnets of this collection arrived suddenly during an intense four-day period, from February 2–5, 1922. He understood them to have come as "a gift," an "inner surge" that he "accepted, purely and obediently."[4] He then turned his full attention to the *Elegies*, completing this epic ten-poem collection over the following ten days, only to be interrupted a second time, from February 15–23, with a further sequence of what became the final twenty-nine sonnets that comprise this work. That final day, with the entire collection in hand, he described their composition with breathless excitement in a letter to his publisher's wife: "Many [came] on a single day, almost simultaneously, such that my pencil was hard-pressed to keep up with their appearance."[5] With minor changes to the poems as he "received" them, these two parts became the *Sonnets to Orpheus* as we now know them. It was a remarkable month of artistic productivity.

These sonnets convey a measure of the same startlement the poet felt in their composition. In a letter written in the month after their publication, in March of 1923, Rilke confessed that "these [sonnets] might strike the reader here and there as somewhat reckless," admitting that "they are perhaps the most secretive—to me first of all, in the manner of their arrival and engagement—and mysterious dictation I have ever endured and achieved."[6] In another letter written a few days later, he went further in acknowledging that he himself did not always understand them: "Much [in them] may be difficult to understand on first or second reading," he conceded, but "with the help of a few explanatory remarks, I can now share them in a way that nothing remains in ambiguous darkness, except for the radiant darkness for which there is no other means [of grasping them] than by an initiation, familiarity, and submission."[7] He warned a trusted friend just before Christmas of that year of the challenges posed by the sonnets' "distillation" and "abbreviation," granting that "much that is in them, given the flow and correlation of the poems, will be accessible only with difficulty."[8]

Rilke sensed early on that these poems marked a turning point in his life following the long inner darkness that had set in with the war and impeded his work as a poet. He addressed that malaise, as part of a wider cultural crisis, in an unsettling poem written the day before the first of these *Sonnets* made their appearance. The abruptness of that poem—with its initial ellipses and the tripling of its opening phrase—reads like a stammering confession of anxiety and dread, opening with these hesitant lines:

> ...When will, when will, when will it suffice,
> the lamenting and declaring? Hadn't the masters at shaping
> human words already come? Why these new attempts?

The poem continues in a similarly despondent vein before concluding with an abrupt and startling shift:

> More than the storms, more than the seas
> have people screamed ... What excess weight of stillness
> would need to inhabit space so that the cricket
> remained audible to us, to us screaming humans. So that the stars
> seemed to us as those keeping silent, in the air we screamed at!

> If only the most distant ones, the old and oldest fathers, might
>   speak to us!
> And we: hearing ones finally! The first hearing people.[9]

This tension of dreadful confusion, on the one hand, and an almost desperate longing, on the other, recalls the opening of what became the first of the *Elegies*, lines he had "received" a decade earlier on a storm-swept January night in 1912. Describing the experience later to his host, Princess Marie Taxis, Rilke spoke of a voice he had heard through the howling winds as he walked alone along the balustrade at the Duino Castle. There, above a cliff path several hundred meters above the Adriatic Sea, he heard this plea: "Who, if I screamed, would hear me among the ranks / of angels?" The *Sonnets* stand as "new attempts" in answer to that cry. He addressed them, however, not to angels as had been the case with the *Elegies*, but to Orpheus, the "singing god" of ancient Greek myths and legends, that "enchanter [who] could make the stones skip, the trees dance, and birds waver in the air."[10]

If these tensions still linger in the sonnets that came a decade later, their message was entirely different. They invite us to embrace life with all its "beauty and terror,"[11] calling us to join Orpheus in indwelling the Earth singing. Ours is work we share with this "lost god" as we learn to face "the open end" that is ever before us:

> We're keen in wanting to know,
> but Orpheus is bright and spread about.
>
> He doesn't take the pure, the consecrated
> offering into his world
> in any other way than by standing,
> unmoved, across from the open end. (II.16)[12]

The *Sonnets* give voice to Rilke's conviction that our vocation as humans is not that of *knowing*, which in one sense is both too much and not enough. It is, rather, that of *experiencing* life's fullness, of opening ourselves to embrace this abundance despite the suffering and losses we must endure.

These poems stand in response to the tensions he had experienced during the decade preceding their composition. They invite us to face death as part of that "open end," and to do it courageously—as Orpheus did—as part of life. They call us to keep our attention on the "here-and-now" of life without seeking to escape into a false transcendence. Indeed, Rilke later described the "two innermost experiences [that] were decisive for writing the *Sonnets*: the soul's growing resolution to hold life open to death, and, on the other side, the spiritual need to set the transformations of love within an expanded 'Whole,' differently than happens in a narrower cycle of life which simply excludes death as 'the other.'"[13] To embrace death as part of life was what he came to see as "the conclusive affirmation" of life's "wholeness," grounding it in the Earth's natural rhythms.

The poems that form the *Elegies* and *Sonnets*, "filled with the same essence" and arriving from "the same birth"[14] as he later put it, joined in this "life-and death-affirmation," since ultimately "there is neither a 'this-side' nor a 'beyond,' but rather [a] great unity."[15] This mystery of "the Whole" of that unity brought Rilke to Orpheus who faced the anguish of death twice-over: first, with the loss of his beloved Eurydice at her death; and second, after he had wooed her back from the Underworld with his song, but then, doubting, turned to see if she still followed behind him—and lost her forever. Over and over these sonnets affirm the indissoluble wholeness of death and life, celebrating love's gains alongside its losses within that overarching unity. Against the pressures of despair, they risk claiming that "everything is distant –, and nowhere does the circle close" (II.20). In all this, they remind us that Orpheus' story, with its fragile and fraught vulnerabilities, is not unlike our own.

❋ ❋ ❋

When I first encountered these poems many years ago, I found them baffling and alluring at once. I have since discovered that this reaction is not uncommon among readers. The strangeness of Rilke's metaphors can be difficult to grasp, and even off-putting, as in the first of the sonnets where the poet exclaims "O tall tree in the ear!" (I.1). Yet perhaps for that very reason I came to discover that such images rooted themselves in the deep recesses of my mind. They seemed to want to linger in the caverns of my imagination. How could I—or anyone, for that matter—experience a "felt" meadow or imagine someone having "slept the world" (I.2)? What would it mean, I wondered, to "follow" Orpheus—or anyone else, for that matter—"through the narrow lyre" (I.3)? And though it was easy enough for me, in my early twenties, to recognize what it meant to have a "divided" mind, what did Rilke intend when he wrote of coming to "the crossroads of two heart-ways," and what was a "heart-way," anyway, where "no temple for Apollo" (I.3) could be found? And when the poet admonishes us not to fear suffering (I.4), I found myself wondering what else one could possibly do in the face of such burdens.

Over the years that followed such questions remained, but that sense of "the Whole" woven through the *Sonnets* began to open me to an unexpected wisdom, one capable of embracing death as part of life, with all its anguish and delight. I began to realize that living into the abundances of this life, of which death is a part, had more to do with trust than certainty. Rilke's admonition to "erect no monument" to Orpheus, but to "just let the rose / bloom each year for his sake" (I.5), pressed toward that "new boundary-line for the realm of what can hardly be said," as von Hofmannsthal had put it. Despite all that seemed destined to discourage or even defeat me, I began to hear these poems giving voice to a bold "nonetheless":

> But life is still enchanted for us; in a hundred
> places it is still a source. A playing of pure
> powers that no one touches who does not kneel and marvel. (II.10)

Such images, of course, are not always easily accessible. As with all deep insight, they come to do their work slowly within us, reaching into the realm of the imagination as we read and reread them—and as they begin to "read" us. After all, the roses that awaken us with the sweet persistence of their scent surpass the reach of "monuments." In their irresistible allure they gesture year after year toward an "unsayable" beauty we long to experience, and with their persistence they embody the unending rhythm of seasons that come and go and come again. Over time I found myself falling under the spell of images like these from the *Sonnets*. The enchantment they evoked began to engage me not for some hoped-for clarity of expression, but rather through the allurement of that "playing of pure powers" they gesture toward, reaching as it does beyond cognition into the depths of the unconscious.

Little by little I found these poems engaging me not as "posts that must be lined up to effect some result," as Rilke once put it, but rather as "a lyric whole" that works through "the inspiration of a similar orientation."[16] For as he admits in one of the early sonnets, "to sing truthfully is a different breath. / A breath about nothing. A blowing in god. A wind." (I.3). In such apparently purposeless wanderings, the sonnets remind us of the "wholeness" we yearn for: "Hail to the spirit that can join us..." (I.12). They also allure us with the expansiveness of their images: "But the winds ... but the spaces ..." (I.4).[17] By such means they beckon us to become what the poet calls "the ones who hear and are a mouth of nature" (I.26).

How, then, are we to listen to these sonnets, and what will we hear in them when we do? Here, a word of both caution and invitation is in order: these poems call for a patient and inquisitive reading, a challenge in a culture like ours that is so often impatient and drawn to the declarative. Rilke already felt this, writing with a lyric style that prizes what does *not* yield easily to our demand for comprehension. These sonnets invite a long listening and a deep lingering. They remind us that what opens us to the depths often lies at the edges of our understanding. Rilke seems to intuit that precisely at the boundary of the "unsayable" we might yet find the vision we most need to receive, an orientation in life that we may have long yearned for without even knowing it. Perhaps for that reason the experience of reading these poems evokes the sense that the poet has refused to open all the doors of comprehension as we might have expected or desired him to do. And while knocking on those closed doors might not cause them to open immediately, our persistence in doing so might lead us beyond what we already know, or thought we needed to know, to find our way into the mysterious depths of our lives.

These poems require, then, a slow and persistent reading. They lure us often because of their strangeness, and not on account of their clarities. Rilke's unpredictable and often highly inventive word-choice, even for German readers, can be challenging to the point of maddening. His diction often seems bent on deliberately puzzling, and his syntax as shaped by what he himself described as "distillations" and "abbreviations" that defy an easy accessibility. Given the inventive possibilities inherent in German as an inflected language, the poet is able to construct phrases and lines layered with complex subordinate clauses, constructions that can only be unraveled with deliberate care. They express the sense of wandering that entering a maze requires. Rilke is aware of this, of course, lamenting in one of these sonnets that we are no longer those who "lay out the paths as a lovely meandering" but rather insist on making them "straight ones" (I.24).

The *Sonnets* seem made for the experience of meandering, resisting a direct manner of approach. They lure and sometimes confuse us with language that does not yield to immediate comprehension. His voice calls us to pause in our restless need to control, to linger with the unfamiliar, to consider the unknown. The sonnets invite us to wander along paths we might not have expected to traverse, to give ourselves over to being startled by unexpected phrases, incomprehensible images, and invented words. They impede our rush for what is straightforward, often bending normal diction even to the point of breaking established grammatical rules. They baffle us with such tendencies, but perhaps that very startlement is what draws us with the poet toward the "unsayable"—to recall a word he frequently employed in the *Sonnets* and later *Elegies*. In all this they beckon us to listen deeply to a voice not our own, to resist our impatient need for meaning and give ourselves over to the meandering ways of the imagination. And, above all, they invite us to "look"—a common verb Rilke often employs in the imperative voice here—for what we can only dimly "sense" at the boundary of language.

The difficulties posed by Rilke's style in these poems is clear enough for German readers. For this very reason, of course, a faithful translation must convey something of the experience of disorientation, defamiliarization, and a corresponding uncertainty. It must risk conveying the essential strangeness inherent in the poet's language. Many of the otherwise commendable English versions of the *Sonnets* refuse this gamble, in part or entirely, choosing safer paths that tame the poems, that flatten their complicated diction and ignore the wildness of their voice. After all, we too prefer the "straight" paths, both as translators and as readers. And while Rilke's poetic lines swing in often dazzlingly lyric arcs, the inventive diction, neologisms, and torqued syntax that comprise these sonnets make for anything but straightforward reading. His lyricism is complex but rarely clever, and I've often felt while lingering with these sonnets that Rilke's intention with them is to bring us to "an entrance whose doorjambs tremble" (I.1), to invite us to reach for what we can sense—if at all—only at the edges of language, to lure us into the enchantment of "being-here."

❋ ❋ ❋

Rilke sensed that we must find a way "beyond the old repressions. . .that have taken the mysteries from us, leaving us increasingly alienated from the fullness by which we might otherwise have lived."[18] Only as we discover traces of these mysteries—in nature and within our own lives—are we able to find our way toward that "open end" we long to face. But he insisted that this path called us to embrace the paradoxical "whole" that binds the "sweet" and "wonderful" with the "terrible" and "dreadful": "Whoever does not accept at some time the dreadfulness [*Fürchterlichkeit*] of life with a firm resolve, even to the point of rejoicing in it, will never possess the unsayable power of our being and will pass to the margins."[19] We come to grasp these mysteries, or find ourselves grasped by them, not in momentous revelations or through dramatic discoveries but rather quietly and unobtrusively as "with words and gestures, little by little, / *we* make the world our own" (I.16).

    As I came face to face with that "dreadfulness" during a long season of loss and loneliness these sonnets were among the voices I turned to and came to trust. Over time, their presence has offered encouragement to the point that I came to sense what Rilke might have meant when he spoke of

> . . . all those rescued
> from doubt, their mouths opened again
> who already knew what keeping silent means. (I.10)

This was a poet whose vision I came to rely upon in my own doubt. His voice in these sonnets does not offer itself as a guide with a ready-made itinerary, or as a peddler of some quick fix for life's difficulties, but as a witness to what it meant—and means—to live with curiosity toward the "mysteries" and compassion toward oneself and others. "Little by little," with "words and gestures," they opened me to recognize the brokenness of my own life as belonging to "the Whole," as part of a larger unity that holds us all and all things. They even began to open within me a glimpse of that "radiant darkness" Rilke wrote of in describing the *Sonnets*, finding its illumining shape within the shadows of loss and the dark pit of anguish. And I began to appreciate how these poems needed time and space to find their voice within me:

> Boys, o don't throw
> your courage into speed,
> into the attempt to fly. (I.22)

After all, these sonnets are resonant with a wisdom Rilke described in the Ninth Elegy as coming from "pain" and "difficulties," which is to say, from "the long experience of love."

They also came to stand for him as "a grave-memorial" for a young woman his daughter's age, Vera Ouckama Knoop. Since early childhood she had been a remarkable dancer, and when she began to lose her physical abilities with the onset of leukemia as she entered puberty, she turned her creative energies to music and writing. Two of the poems address her directly (I.25 and II.28), and others—among them, I.2 and II.12—seem to be written in homage to the courage and creativity she embodied in the face of the debilitating suffering she faced. He opened the latter with a call:

> Desire the change. O be enthralled with the flame
> in which a thing withdraws from you that brims with
>   transformations;
> that shaping spirit, which masters the earthly,
> loves in the figure's swing nothing as much as the turning point. (II.12)

Rilke knew that our resilience in the face of hardships, and not our accomplishments, is what most mattered. Not the goal to be achieved but the "turning points" in our experience are what creativity depends upon and offers. As he put it in a letter written several years earlier, "If [your] angel condescends to come, it will be because you have persuaded him, not with your tears, but by your humble decision to start afresh: *to be a beginner!*"[20]

❋ ❋ ❋

The *Sonnets* came to Rilke in what should have been midlife, when he was forty-six years old, though at the time he was already beginning to feel the onset of the disease that led to his death less than five years later. They describe what felt to him like "a new beginning, a sign, and change" (I.1), an awakening that he found mirrored in his deepening interest in Orpheus. At the time he kept a picture of the "singing god"—a postcard depicting an engraving by a Renaissance artist—pinned to the wall above his writing desk at Muzot. That image portrayed "the god [who] is the place that heals" (II.16) sitting against a tree—"There a tree arose! O pure transcending! / O Orpheus is singing! O tall tree in the ear!"—as he played the lyre, enchanting the animals circled around him. The contrast of his alluring song, as Rilke presents it in this collection, stands in stark contrast to the pressures of modern life, which left many restless, unsatisfied and driven by ambition:

> We are the achievers.
> But this march of time,
> consider it a trifle
> among what ever abides.
>
> All that hastens
> will soon be gone,
> for what lingers
> first consecrates us. (I.22)

Hastening and lingering, the restlessness of movement and the stillness of presence, transience and eternity: these are the binaries, according to Rilke's sensibilities, that burden us. But he also knew them as "pure tensions" that could open us to a deeper life. These are what led him to invoke Orpheus and his gift: "O music of the powers!" (I.12). This god's saving gift, then, is nothing other than his song. What opens us to receiving it is our loneliness and lostness, the "dread" and "terror" that awaken us to the unitive forces of our lives: "Hail to the spirit that can join us together, / for we live truly in figures" (I.12).

Although Rilke occasionally identifies Orpheus as "master" (*Herr*) here,[21] he generally addressed him directly as "you," using the intimate second-person German pronoun *du*. We find this already in the opening sonnet. After speaking *about* Orpheus in the third-person in the initial stanza—"O Orpheus is singing!"—he turns to address him directly in the closing line, "You built temples for them in their hearing." The same voice is found in the later sonnets when the poet addresses this "you" as the "singing god" (I.2 and II.26), the teacher of song (I.3), and the "lost god" (I.26).[22] But what we find as early as the fourth sonnet in this cycle—"O you tender ones" and "O you who are blessed, o you who are whole"—signals a subtle but important change in the poet's use of the second-person imperative: Rilke shifts already at an early point in this poem-cycle from addressing Orpheus to addressing us—in the plural—as readers.[23] Thus, the "singing god" recedes not only into silence but into invisibility as the cycle unfolds, and in his place we discover ourselves as those listening for the last traces of his song: "O you lost god! O you unending trace!" (I.26). In the silence of our listening we witness Orpheus' absent presence and become heirs to his song—which is "Being" itself (I.3).

Rilke uses this same direct voice when he addresses *things* as "you," rather than simply talking *about* them as inanimate objects, as we are prone to do.[24] This feature emerges most persistently in the poems that became the second part of the collection: "You... breath" (II.1), "you... rose" (II.6), "you... fountain-mouth" (II.15), and so on. This style mirrors Orpheus' role in embracing the disordered world by singing its creatures and things into harmony with each other. His music binds separated things together as parts—with us—of "the Whole." As we find his song becoming our own, we hear him calling us to "speak and bear witness," as he put it in the Ninth Elegy, inviting us to take Orpheus' vision as our own. We are the ones summoned to embrace his role and sing where he had fallen silent: "Once and for all / it's Orpheus when there's singing" (I.5). Ours is the Orphic song offered now in the absence of the one "who still, deep in the doors of the dead, / holds bowls filled with praiseworthy fruits" (I.7).

Over the arc of these sonnets, Rilke's "you" thus comes to address us as readers. He makes this shift clear by depicting Orpheus—subtly at first, but with increasing persistence as the cycle unfolds—in the third person, as an increasingly silent memory. We eventually come to stand face-to-face with this remembered but absent god; in so doing, we find ourselves wondering, as the poet does, about what new fullness we might make room for in *our* listening—as in our singing. Here, the contrast to the "machine" becomes central, a "made" thing that itself "wants to be praised now" despite its noise and the turbulence it creates:

> Consider the machine:
> how it writhes and avenges
> and contorts and depletes us.
>
> Even if it derives its power from us,
> let it passionlessly
> work and serve. (I.18)

And, as he puts it in a later sonnet, the machine misguidedly imagines that

> The machine is life —, it thinks it can do it best,
> ordering and creating and destroying with the same resolve. (II.10)

Will we turn toward "the machine," embodying as it does the perils of automation that threatened modernity, as Rilke came to understand it? Or will we return to the world we once inhabited, naturally and joyfully, as children? And when, in one of the last sonnets, we hear the invitation to "Sing the gardens, my heart, that you don't know" (II.21), we find Rilke beckoning us to assume the role of the "lost god":

> Only because this enmity in the end scattered you in rage
> are we now the ones who hear and are a mouth of nature. (I.26)

We thus come to find ourselves standing as Orpheus' heirs who live to "speak and bear witness" with our lives to the truth that "song is Being" (I.5).

※ ※ ※

One of the central threads woven through these sonnets, finally, is the theme of praise. The opening of one of the early poems announces this boldly:

> To praise, that's it! As one appointed to praise,
> [Orpheus] came forth like ore from the stone's
> silence. (I.7)

Whom or what should we praise, as Orpheus had been "appointed" to do? Rilke refuses to identify the object of praise with a transcendent being, whether Orpheus or some other "god"—or any other figure, for that matter. Our praise is for what is "here-and-now" among us—*das Hiesige*, to recall a word he favors in the *Sonnets* and *Elegies*—and not for something beyond us (*jenseits*). Nor are we to praise Orpheus as if he were different from us or somehow "higher" than we are. For our work like his is to praise what is present, in life and in death. In response to the question posed at the outset of the Ninth Elegy where the poet wonders why we are here, he answers:

> But because being-here matters so much, and because
> all that is here-and-now [*das Hiesige*] seemingly needs us, this
>   fleetingness that
> strangely concerns us. Us, the most fleeting of all.

This is Rilke's hymn to presence, his call to live into a measure of life's fullness, to indwell its "hereness," however fragmented and anguishing that might seem to us. But he was intent on reminding us that this is not Orpheus' work alone. It falls to us to discover that we, as "silken thread," are "woven into the weave," that every moment of our lives, with all the anguish and sorrows we face, is part of "the whole, the praiseworthy carpet" (II.21).

How we learn to do this, given the loneliness and losses we must face, is one of the poet's overriding concerns in this poem-cycle. It is the same message we hear resounding with an equal urgency throughout the *Elegies*, but particularly in the Eighth and Ninth—written between his completion over a matter of weeks of the two parts of the *Sonnets*, which is why I have included them in this volume. He warns us in them, with a more direct voice than in the *Sonnets* with their beguiling lyricism, of the difficulties that tempt us to turn from the source of life's "abundance," often hidden in the simple "hereness" of things. When we fall to this temptation, we relinquish our sense of participating in this world and become mere observers of our own lives as he declares near the close of the Eighth Elegy:

> And we: spectators, always, everywhere,
> turned toward it all and never looking out!

The *Sonnets* explore this plight with a different voice than we hear in the

Elegies, but their message is no different: they invite us to know that "song is Being," and to come to experience how it is that we belong to "the Whole" amid what we experience as our limitations and insufficiencies. This is the insight that shapes these poems, voicing in "words and gestures" and the silences surrounding them what he had spoken of as "the spiritual need to set the transformations of love. . .within an expanded 'Whole.'"[25]

In gaining a sense that this is the heart of our lives, we discover with Rilke that we should not look back but ahead—in the presence of all that we must ultimately let go of in death:

> Be ahead of all parting, as if it were behind
> you like the winter now passing.
> For among winters there is one so endlessly winter
> that in overwintering it your heart just survives. (II.13)

The *Sonnets* presume that we are made not merely to *survive* an "endless" winter, but to *thrive* through our embracing "the realm of what is barely sayable." These poems offer glimpses of that "radiant darkness" we carry within us. They call us to "speak and bear witness" since "more than ever, / things that can be experienced fall apart," as he put it in the Ninth Elegy. They remind us to embrace the conviction that

> Only the song, over the land,
> hallows and celebrates. (I.19)

Ours is the work of listening for this song as it "hallows" *us*. For as we begin to hear it, we find ourselves invited into that sense of "the Whole," with all the disorder we experience around us and the disappointments within. This is the temple Orpheus still builds "for our hearing," and it is in this hearing that we live into the "mysteries" and find, in our own lives, a sense of the "fullness" we long for. This is what it means to discover that "it's Orpheus when there's singing," and enter that song, not with declarations or demands but with listening and longing. This is what it means to live in praise.

SONNETS

TO

ORPHEUS

written as a grave-memorial
for Vera Ouckama Knoop

DIE

SONETTE

AN

ORPHEUS

geschrieben als ein Grab-Mal
für Wera Ouckama Knoop

*

CHÂTEAU DE MUZOT
IN
FEBRUARY, 1922
INSEL VERLAG, 1923

FIRST PART

1

Da stieg ein Baum. O reine Übersteigung!
O Orpheus singt! O hoher Baum im Ohr!
Und alles schwieg. Doch selbst in der Verschweigung
ging neuer Anfang, Wink und Wandlung vor.

Tiere aus Stille drangen aus dem klaren
gelösten Wald von Lager und Genist;
und da ergab sich, daß sie nicht aus List
und nicht aus Angst in sich so leise waren,

sondern aus Hören. Brüllen, Schrei, Geröhr
schien klein in ihren Herzen. Und wo eben
kaum eine Hütte war, dies zu empfangen,

ein Unterschlupf aus dunkelstem Verlangen
mit einem Zugang, dessen Pfosten beben, –
da schufst du ihnen Tempel im Gehör.

1

There a tree arose. O pure transcending!
O Orpheus is singing! O tall tree in the ear!
And everything kept still. But even in this stillness
a new beginning, sign, and change came forth.

Creatures of stillness thronged from their lairs
and nests out of the clear and spacious forest,
and they became so quiet in themselves,
not from cunning and not from fear

but from listening. Bellowing, screaming, roaring
seemed small in their hearts. And there
where a meager hut stood to take all this in,

a refuge made of darkest desires
with an entrance whose doorjambs tremble, –
you built temples for them in their hearing.

2

Und fast ein Mädchen wars und ging hervor
aus diesem einigen Glück von Sang und Leier
und glänzte klar durch ihre Frühlingsschleier
und machte sich ein Bett in meinem Ohr.

Und schlief in mir. Und alles war ihr Schlaf.
Die Bäume, die ich je bewundert, diese
fühlbare Ferne, die gefühlte Wiese
und jedes Staunen, das mich selbst betraf.

Sie schlief die Welt. Singender Gott, wie hast
du sie vollendet, daß sie nicht begehrte,
erst wach zu sein? Sieh, sie erstand und schlief.

Wo ist ihr Tod? O wirst du dies Motiv
erfinden noch, eh sich dein Lied verzehrte? –
Wo sinkt sie hin aus mir? . . . Ein Mädchen fast . . . .

2

And almost a girl it was who came forth
from this twinned delight of song and lyre,
who shone brightly through her springtide veil
and made her bed within my ear.

And slept within me. And her sleep was everything.
The trees I'd always admired, this
palpable distance, the meadow I'd felt,
and each amazement that touched me.

She slept the world. Singing god, how did you
so perfect her that she did not desire
first to be awake? Look, she arose and then slept.

Where is her death? O, will you yet invent
this motif before your song expires? –
Where does she sink to from within me? . . . Almost a girl . . . .

3

Ein Gott vermags. Wie aber, sag mir, soll
ein Mann ihm folgen durch die schmale Leier?
Sein Sinn ist Zwiespalt. An der Kreuzung zweier
Herzwege steht kein Tempel für Apoll.

Gesang, wie du ihn lehrst, ist nicht Begehr,
nicht Werbung um ein endlich noch Erreichtes;
Gesang ist Dasein. Für den Gott ein Leichtes.
Wann aber *sind* wir? Und wann wendet *er*

an unser Sein die Erde und die Sterne?
Dies *ists* nicht, Jüngling, daß du liebst, wenn auch
die Stimme dann den Mund dir aufstößt, – lerne

vergessen, daß du aufsangst. Das verrinnt.
In Wahrheit singen, ist ein andrer Hauch.
Ein Hauch um nichts. Ein Wehn im Gott. Ein Wind.

3

A god can do it. But tell me, how should
a man follow him through the narrow lyre?
His mind is divided; at the crossroads of two
heart-ways stands no temple for Apollo.

Song, as you teach it, is not desire,
not a courting of something finally attained.
Song is Being. Something easy for a god.
But when *are* we alive? And when will *he* turn

the Earth and the stars toward our being?
This *isn't it*, young man, that you love, even if
your voice opens your mouth wide, – learn

to forget that you sang out. For this will pass.
To sing truthfully is a different breath.
A breath about nothing. A blowing in god. A wind.

4

O ihr Zärtlichen, tretet zuweilen
in den Atem, der euch nicht meint,
laßt ihn an eueren Wangen sich teilen,
hinter zittert er, wieder vereint.

O ihr Seligen, o ihr Heilen,
die ihr der Anfang der Herzen scheint.
Bogen der Pfeile und Ziele von Pfeilen,
ewiger glänzt euer Lächeln verweint.

Fürchtet Euch nicht zu leiden, die Schwere,
gebt sie zurück an der Erde Gewicht;
schwer sind die Berge, schwer sind die Meere.

Selbst die als Kinder ihr pflanztet, die Bäume,
wurden zu schwer längst; ihr trüget sie nicht.
Aber die Lüfte . . . aber die Räume . . . .

4

O you tender ones, now and then step out
into the breath that isn't about you;
let it part around your cheeks,
and then join again, trembling, behind you.

O you who are blessed, o you who are whole,
who appear to be the origin of hearts.
Bows for the arrows and the arrows' targets,
your tear-soaked smile shines beyond forever.

Don't fear suffering, and give the burdens
back to the Earth's weight;
heavy are the mountains, heavy the seas.

Even the trees you planted as children
became too heavy long ago; you couldn't carry them.
But the winds . . . but the spaces . . . .

5

Errichtet keinen Denkstein. Laßt die Rose
nur jedes Jahr zu seinen Gunsten blühn.
Denn Orpheus ists. Seine Metamorphose
in dem und dem. Wir sollen uns nicht mühn

um andre Namen. Ein für alle Male
ists Orpheus, wenn es singt. Er kommt und geht.
Ists nicht schon viel, wenn er die Rosenschale
um ein paar Tage manchmal übersteht?

O wie er schwinden muß, daß ihrs begrifft!
Und wenn ihm selbst auch bangte, daß er schwände.
Indem sein Wort das Hiersein übertrifft,

ist er schon dort, wohin ihrs nicht begleitet.
Der Leier Gitter zwängt ihm nicht die Hände.
Und er gehorcht, indem er überschreitet.

5

Erect no monument. Just let the rose
bloom each year for his sake.
For it's Orpheus. His metamorphosis
in this and that. We shouldn't trouble ourselves

with other names. Once and for all
it's Orpheus when there's singing. He comes and goes.
Isn't it already enough when he sometimes
outlasts the bowl of roses by a few days?

O that he must fade away for you to grasp this!
Even though he himself feared he would vanish.
When his word exceeds this being-here,

he's already there where you can't accompany him.
The lyre's neck doesn't force his hands.
And he obeys even as he transgresses.

6

Ist er ein Hiesiger? Nein, aus beiden
Reichen erwuchs seine weite Natur.
Kundiger böge die Zweige der Weiden,
wer die Wurzeln der Weiden erfuhr.

Geht ihr zu Bette, so laßt auf dem Tische
Brot nicht und Milch nicht; die Toten ziehts –.
Aber er, der Beschwörende, mische
unter der Milde des Augenlids

ihre Erscheinung in alles Geschaute;
und der Zauber von Erdrauch und Raute
sei ihm so wahr wie der klarste Bezug.

Nichts kann das gültige Bild ihm verschlimmern;
sei es aus Gräbern, sei aus Zimmern,
rühme er Fingerring, Spange und Krug.

6

Is he from around here? No, for his spacious
nature grew out of both realms.
Those who've experienced the willow's roots
bend its branches more adeptly.

When you go to bed, leave no bread on the table
and no milk; this lures the dead –.
But he, the conjurer, let him
mingle their appearance

in all that's seen beneath the eyelid's gentleness;
and may the spell of earth-smoke and rue
be as real for him as the clearest connection.

Nothing can taint the authentic image for him;
whether from graves, whether from rooms,
let him praise finger-ring, clasp, and jug.

7

Rühmen, das ists! Ein zum Rühmen Bestellter,
ging er hervor wie das Erz aus des Steins
Schweigen. Sein Herz, o vergängliche Kelter
eines den Menschen unendlichen Weins.

Nie versagt ihm die Stimme am Staube,
wenn ihn das göttliche Beispiel ergreift.
Alles wird Weinberg, alles wird Traube,
in seinem fühlenden Süden gereift.

Nicht in den Grüften der Könige Moder
straft ihm die Rühmung lügen, oder
daß von den Göttern ein Schatten fällt.

Er ist einer der bleibenden Boten,
der noch weit in die Türen der Toten
Schalen mit rühmlichen Früchten hält.

7

To praise, that's it! As one appointed to praise,
he came forth like ore from the stone's
silence. His heart, o fleeting winepress
of a wine unending for humans.

Never does his voice fail him in the dust
when the divine form seizes him.
Everything becomes vineyard and grapes,
ripened in his sentient south.

Mold of the tombs of kings
doesn't sentence his praise to lie, nor
a shadow that falls from the gods.

He's one of the abiding messengers
who still, deep in the doors of the dead,
holds bowls of praiseworthy fruits.

8

Nur im Raum der Rühmung darf die Klage
gehn, die Nymphe des geweinten Quells,
wachend über unserm Niederschlage,
daß er klar sei an demselben Fels,

der die Tore trägt und die Altäre. –
Sieh, um ihre stillen Schultern früht
das Gefühl, daß sie die jüngste wäre
unter den Geschwistern im Gemüt.

Jubel *weiß*, und Sehnsucht ist geständig, –
nur die Klage lernt noch; mädchenhändig
zählt sie nächtelang das alte Schlimme.

Aber plötzlich, schräg und ungeübt,
hält sie doch ein Sternbild unsrer Stimme
in den Himmel, den ihr Hauch nicht trübt.

8

Only in the realm of praise may lament
go, nymph of the tear-soaked spring,
watching over our downpour
that it falls purely on the same rock

that bears both portals and altars. –
Look, the feeling that she's the youngest
among her soul-siblings dawns
around her quiet shoulders.

Rejoicing *knows* and longing confesses, –
lament alone keeps learning; with girl-like hands
she measures the old wickedness, night after night.

But all at once, askew and unpracticed,
she lifts a constellation of our voice
into the sky, unclouded by her breath.

9

Nur wer die Leier schon hob
auch unter Schatten,
darf das unendliche Lob
ahnend erstatten.

Nur wer mit Toten vom Mohn
aß, von dem ihren,
wird nicht den leisesten Ton
wieder verlieren.

Mag auch die Spieglung im Teich
oft uns verschwimmen:
Wisse das Bild.

Erst in dem Doppelbereich
werden die Stimmen
ewig und mild.

9

Only one who has raised the lyre
even among shadows
may, intuiting, render
unending praise.

Only one who has eaten with the dead
of their own poppy
won't relinquish again
the quietest note.

Even if the pond's reflection
becomes blurred for us:
know the image.

Only in the double-realm
will the voices become
eternal and mild.

10

Euch, die ihr nie mein Gefühl verließt,
grüß ich, antikische Sarkophage,
die das fröhliche Wasser römischer Tage
als ein wandelndes Lied durchfließt.

Oder jene so offenen, wie das Aug
eines frohen erwachenden Hirten,
– innen voll Stille und Bienensaug –
denen entzückte Falter entschwirrten;

alle, die man dem Zweifel entreißt,
grüß ich, die wiedergeöffneten Munde,
die schon wußten, was schweigen heißt.

Wissen wirs, Freunde, wissens wir nicht?
Beides bildet die zögernde Stunde
in dem menschlichen Angesicht.

1 0

I greet you all, ancient sarcophagi,
who never abandoned my feelings,
you through which the glad water of Roman times
flows like a meandering song.

Or those who're so open, like the eye
of a merry waking shepherd
 – full of stillness and dead-nettle within –
from whom enchanted butterflies fluttered forth;

I greet all those rescued from doubt,
their mouths opened again
who already knew what keeping silent means.

Do we know this, friends, or don't we?
Both shape the hesitant hour
within the human face.

11

Sieh den Himmel. Heißt kein Sternbild "Reiter"?
Denn dies ist uns seltsam eingeprägt:
dieser Stolz aus Erde. Und ein Zweiter,
der ihn treibt und hält und den er trägt.

Ist nicht so, gejagt und dann gebändigt,
diese sehnige Natur des Seins?
Weg und Wendung. Doch ein Druck verständigt.
Neue Weite. Und die zwei sind eins.

Aber *sind* sie's? Oder meinen beide
nicht den Weg, den sie zusammen tun?
Namenlos schon trennt sie Tisch und Weide.

Auch die sternische Verbindung trügt.
Doch uns freue eine Weile nun
der Figur zu glauben. Das genügt.

11

Look at the sky. Is no constellation named "Rider"?
For this is strangely imprinted upon us:
this pride of the Earth. And a second one,
who presses and restrains him and whom it bears.

Isn't it so, hunted and then tamed,
this sinewy nature of our being?
Path and turning. Yet a pressing clarifies.
New expanse. And the two are one.

But *are* they? Or don't both suggest
the path that they together take?
Namelessly, table and pasture already divide them.

Even the starry connection deceives.
Yet let us delight for a moment
in believing this figure. That suffices.

12

Heil dem Geist, der uns verbinden mag;
denn wir leben wahrhaft in Figuren.
Und mit kleinen Schritten gehn die Uhren
neben unserm eigentlichen Tag.

Ohne unsern wahren Platz zu kennen,
handeln wir aus wirklichem Bezug.
Die Antennen fühlen die Antennen,
und die leere Ferne trug . . .

Reine Spannung. O Musik der Kräfte!
Ist nicht durch die läßlichen Geschäfte
jede Störung von dir abgelenkt?

Selbst wenn sich der Bauer sorgt und handelt,
wo die Saat in Sommer sich verwandelt,
reicht er niemals hin. Die Erde *schenkt.*

12

Hail to the spirit that can join us,
for we truly live in figures.
And the clocks move in small steps
alongside our own day.

Without recognizing our true place
we act in genuine accord.
Antennae sense antennae,
and the empty distance carried . . .

Pure tension. O music of the powers!
Isn't it so that our unneeded tasks
deflect every disturbance from you?

Even if the farmer worries and works,
he never reaches the place where seed transforms
itself into summer. The Earth *gifts*.

13

Voller Apfel, Birne und Banane,
Stachelbeere ... Alles dieses spricht
Tod und Leben in den Mund ... Ich ahne ...
Lest es einem Kind vom Angesicht,

wenn es sie erschmeckt. Dies kommt von weit.
Wird euch langsam namenlos im Munde?
Wo sonst Worte waren, fließen Funde,
aus dem Fruchtfleisch überrascht befreit.

Wagt zu sagen, was ihr Apfel nennt.
Diese Süße, die sich erst verdichtet,
um, im Schmecken leise aufgerichtet,

klar zu werden, wach und transparent,
doppeldeutig, sonnig, erdig, hiesig –:
O Erfahrung, Fühlung, Freude –, riesig!

13

Fullness of apple, pear and banana,
gooseberry . . . All this speaks
death and life in the mouth . . . I sense . . .
Read it on a child's face

when it tastes them. This comes from afar.
Is it being slowly rendered nameless in your mouth?
Where words once were discoveries now flow,
startled in being freed from the fruit's flesh.

Dare to say what you call apple.
This sweetness that first intensifies
so that, quietly formed in our tasting,

it becomes clear, alert, and transparent,
ambiguous, sunny, earthy, present –:
O experience, sensation, joy –, immense!

14

Wir gehen um mit Blume, Weinblatt, Frucht.
Sie sprechen nicht die Sprache nur des Jahres.
Aus Dunkel steigt ein buntes Offenbares
und hat vielleicht den Glanz der Eifersucht

der Toten an sich, die die Erde stärken.
Was wissen wir von ihrem Teil an dem?
Es ist seit lange ihre Art, den Lehm
mit ihrem freien Marke zu durchmärken.

Nun fragt sich nur: tun sie es gern? . . .
Drängt diese Frucht, ein Werk von schweren Sklaven,
geballt zu uns empor, zu ihren Herrn?

Sind *sie* die Herrn, die bei den Wurzel schlafen,
und gönnen uns aus ihren Überflüssen
dies Zwischending aus stummer Kraft und Küssen?

14

We occupy ourselves with flowers, vine leaves, fruit.
They don't just speak the language of the year.
A colorful revealing rises from the dark
and has something of the shine of the jealousy

of the dead who strengthen the Earth.
What do we know of their part in this?
It's long been their way to marrow the loam
all the way through with their own free marrow.

Now the only question is: do they do this gladly? . . .
Does this fruit, a work of strong slaves,
press up, clenched, to us, their masters?

Or are *they* the masters who sleep among the roots,
indulging us out of their abundances
this in-between-thing made of mute power and kisses?

15

Wartet . . ., das schmeckt . . . Schon ists auf der Flucht.
. . . . Wenig Musik nur, ein Stampfen, ein Summen –:
Mädchen, ihr warmen, Mädchen, ihr stummen,
tanzt den Geschmack der erfahrenen Frucht!

Tanzt die Orange. Wer kann sie vergessen,
wie sie, ertrinkend in sich, sich wehrt
wider ihr Süßsein. Ihr habt sie besessen.
Sie hat sich köstlich zu euch bekehrt.

Tanzt die Orange. Die wärmere Landschaft,
werft sie aus euch, daß die reife erstrahle
in Lüften der Heimat! Erglühte, enthüllt

Düfte um Düfte! Schafft die Verwandtschaft
mit der reinen, sich weigernden Schale,
mit dem Saft, der die Glückliche füllt!

15

Wait . . ., that's delicious . . . Already it's on the run.
. . . . Just a bit of music, a stamping, a hum –:
girls, you who're warm, girls, you who're mute,
dance the savor of the fruit you've tasted!

Dance the orange. Who can forget this,
how, drowning in itself, it defends itself
against its own sweetness. You've possessed it.
It has converted itself deliciously toward you.

Dance the orange. The warmer landscape,
throw it forth from within you so that the ripe orange might shine
in your homeland's winds! In its glowing it unveils

fragrance upon fragrance. Establish kinship
with the pure, resisting rind,
with the juice that fills the happy fruit!

16

Du, mein Freund, bist einsam, weil . . . .
Wir machen mit Worten und Fingerzeigen
uns allmählich die Welt zu eigen,
vielleicht ihren schwächsten, gefährlichsten Teil.

Wer zeigt mit Fingern auf einen Geruch? –
Doch von den Kräften, die uns bedrohten,
fühlst du viele . . . Du kennst die Toten,
und du erschrickst vor dem Zauberspruch.

Sieh, nun heißt es zusammen ertragen
Stückwerk und Teile, als sei es das Ganze.
Dir helfen, wird schwer sein. Vor allem: pflanze

mich nicht in dein Herz. Ich wüchse zu schnell.
Doch *meines* Herrn Hand will ich führen und sagen:
Hier. Das ist Esau in seinem Fell.

16

You, my friend, are lonely, because . . . .
With words and gestures, little by little,
we make the world our own,
perhaps its weakest and most hazardous part.

Who points fingers at a smell?
Yet you feel many of the forces
that threatened us . . . You know the dead
and you're frightened by their magic spell.

Look, now we must together bear
piecework and parts as if this were the whole.
To help you will be hard. Above all: don't plant

me in your heart. I'd grow too quickly.
Yet I'll lead *my* master's hand and say:
Here. That's Esau in his fleece.

17

Zu unterst der Alte, verworrn,
all der Erbauten
Wurzel, verborgener Born,
den sie nie schauten.

Sturmhelm und Jägerhorn,
Spruch von Ergrauten,
Männer im Bruderzorn,
Frauen wie Lauten . . .

Drängender Zweig an Zweig,
nirgends ein freier . . . .
Einer! O steig . . . o steig . . .

Aber sie brechen noch.
Dieser erst oben doch
biegt sich zur Leier.

17

Beneath it all, the old muddled one,
root of all that's been
built, hidden spring
which they've never seen.

Battle-helmet and hunter's horn,
a saying of the elders,
men driven by brotherly wrath,
women like lutes . . . .

Branch pressing on branch,
and nowhere a free one . . .
One! O climb . . . o climb . . .

But they will yet break.
The one at the top, though,
bends itself into a lyre.

18

Hörst du das Neue, Herr,
dröhnen und beben?
Kommen Verkündiger,
die es erheben.

Zwar ist kein Hören heil
in dem Durchtobtsein,
doch der Maschinenteil
will jetzt gelobt sein.

Sieh, die Maschine:
wie sie sich wälzt und rächt
und uns entstellt und schwächt.

Hat sie aus uns auch Kraft,
sie, ohne Leidenschaft,
treibe und diene.

18

Do you hear the new, master,
roaring and quaking?
Heralds come
to exalt it.

For though no one can hear
amid this turbulence,
the machine still
wants to be praised now.

Consider the machine:
how it writhes and avenges
and contorts and depletes us.

Even if it derives its power from us,
let it passionlessly
work and serve.

19

Wandelt sich rasch auch die Welt
wie Wolkengestalten,
alles Vollendete fällt
heim zum Uralten.

Über dem Wandel und Gang,
weiter und freier,
währt noch dein Vor-Gesang,
Gott mit der Leier.

Nicht sind die Leiden erkannt,
nicht ist die Liebe gelernt,
und was im Tod uns entfernt,

ist nicht entschleiert.
Einzig das Lied überm Land
heiligt und feiert.

19

Though the world changes as swiftly
as cloud-forms,
all that's perfected returns
home to the most ancient of things.

Beyond the change and passing,
farther and freer,
your primal song endures,
god with the lyre.

Suffering has not been understood,
nor has love been learned,
and what distances us in death

is not unveiled.
Only the song, over the land,
hallows and celebrates.

20

Dir aber, Herr, o was weih ich dir, sag,
der das Ohr den Geschöpfen gelehrt? –
Mein Erinnern an einen Frühlingstag,
seinen Abend, in Rußland –, ein Pferd . . .

Herüber vom Dorf kam der Schimmel allein,
an der vorderen Fessel den Pflock,
um die Nacht auf den Wiesen allein zu sein;
wie schlug der Mähne Gelock

an den Hals im Takte des Übermuts,
bei dem grob gehemmten Galopp.
Wie sprangen die Quellen des Rossebluts!

Der fühlte die Weiten, und ob!
Der sang und der hörte –, dein Sagenkreis
war *in* ihm geschlossen.
$\qquad\qquad$ Sein Bild: ich weih's.

20

To you, master, o what should I consecrate to you, tell,
who taught the creatures' ear?
My remembering of a spring day,
one evening, in Russia –, a horse . . .

From the village, a white steed approached, alone,
a hobble affixed to his front ankle
to bind him in the night, alone, on the meadows;
how the locks of his mane stroked

his neck in keeping with his high spirit,
with that clumsily hindered gallop.
How the springs of the stallion's blood leaped!

He sensed the distances, and how!
He sang and he listened –, your legend's cycle
became enclosed *within* him.

His image: I consecrate it.

21

Frühling ist wiedergekommen. Die Erde
ist wie ein Kind, das Gedichte weiß;
viele, o viele . . . . Für die Beschwerde
langen Lernens bekommt sie den Preis.

Streng war ihr Lehrer. Wir mochten das Weiße
an dem Barte des alten Manns.
Nun, wie das Grüne, das Blaue heiße,
dürfen wir fragen: sie kanns, sie kanns!

Erde, die frei hat, du glückliche, spiele
nun mit den Kindern. Wir wollen dich fangen,
fröhliche Erde. Dem Frohsten gelingts.

O, was der Lehrer sie lehrte, das Viele,
und was gedruckt steht in Wurzeln und langen
schwierigen Stämmen: sie singts, sie singts!

21

Spring has returned. The Earth
is like a child who knows poems;
many, o many . . . . For the trouble
of long learning she takes the prize.

Strict was her teacher. We liked the white
of the old man's beard.
Now, we may ask what the green, what the blue
could mean: she can do it, she can do it!

Earth, on holiday, you lucky one, play
now with the children. We want to catch you,
glad Earth. The happiest succeed at this.

O, what the teacher taught her, much as it was,
and what's been imprinted in roots and the long
complicated stems: she sings it, she sings it!

22

Wir sind die Treibenden.
Aber den Schritt der Zeit,
nehmt ihn als Kleinigkeit
im immer Bleibenden.

Alles das Eilende
wird schon vorüber sein;
denn das Verweilende
erst weiht uns ein.

Knaben, o werft den Mut
nicht in die Schnelligkeit,
nicht in den Flugversuch.

Alles ist ausgeruht:
Dunkel und Helligkeit,
Blume und Buch.

2 2

We are the achievers.
But this march of time,
consider it a trifle
among what ever abides.

All that hastens
will soon be gone,
for what lingers
first consecrates us.

Boys, o don't throw
your courage into speed,
into the attempt to fly.

Everything is at rest:
darkness and bright,
blossom and book.

23

O erst *dann*, wenn der Flug
nicht mehr um seinetwillen
wird in die Himmelstillen
steigen, sich selber genug,

um in lichten Profilen,
als das Gerät, das gelang,
Liebling der Winde zu spielen,
sicher, schwenkend und schlank, –

erst, wenn ein reines Wohin
wachsender Apparate
Knabenstolz überwiegt,

wird, überstürzt von Gewinn,
jener den Fernen Genahte
sein, was er einsam erfliegt.

23

O only *then* when flight
no longer climbs for its own sake,
self-sufficiently,
into stillnesses of sky,

that in thin profiles
as the tool that succeeded
in playing darling to the winds,
securely swaying and slender, –

only when a pure whither
of advancing devices
outweighs boyhood pride

will that one, pressed by the zeal to win,
having come near from over the distances,
be what he attains in solitary flight.

24

Sollen wir unsere uralte Freundschaft, die großen
niemals werbenden Götter, weil sie der harte
Stahl, den wir streng erzogen, nicht kennt, verstoßen
oder sie plötzlich suchen auf einer Karte?

Diese gewaltigen Freunde, die uns die Toten
nehmen, rühren nirgends an unsere Räder.
Unsere Gastmähler haben wir weit –, unsere Bäder,
fortgerückt, und ihre uns lang schon zu langsamen Boten

überholen wir immer. Einsamer nun auf einander
ganz angewiesen, ohne einander zu kennen,
führen wir nicht mehr die Pfade als schöne Mäander,

sondern als Grade. Nur noch in Dampfkesseln brennen
die einstigen Feuer und heben die Hämmer, die immer
größern. Wir aber nehmen an Kraft ab, wie Schwimmer.

2 4

Should we renounce our ancient friendship with the great
never-courting gods because the hard
steel we diligently fashioned doesn't recognize them,
or should we suddenly search for them on a map?

These powerful friends who take the dead
from us nowhere stir against our wheels.
We've removed our banquets and our baths
to places far off, and we always overtake their messengers

who've long been too slow for us. Lonelier now, reliant
entirely on each other without knowing who we are,
we no longer lay out the paths as a lovely meandering

but in straight lines. Only in the steam boilers do the fires
of long ago still burn, now driving ever-larger pistons.
Yet we diminish in strength like swimmers.

25

Dich aber will ich nun, *Dich*, die ich kannte
wie eine Blume, von der ich den Namen nicht weiß,
noch *ein* Mal erinnern und ihnen zeigen, Entwandte,
schöne Gespielin des unüberwindlichen Schrei's.

Tänzerin erst, die plötzlich, den Körper voll Zögern,
anhielt, als göß man ihr Jungsein in Erz;
trauernd und lauschend –. Da, von den hohen Vermögern
fiel ihr Musik in das veränderte Herz.

Nah war die Krankheit. Schon von den Schatten bemächtigt,
drängte verdunkelt das Blut, doch, wie flüchtig verdächtigt,
trieb es in seinen natürlichen Frühling hervor.

Wieder und wieder, von Dunkel und Sturz unterbrochen,
glänzte es irdisch. Bis es nach schrecklichem Pochen
trat in das trostlos offene Tor.

25

I want to remember *you* now, *you* whom I knew
like a flower whose name I didn't know;
I want to remember you *once* more, and show you to them as
one stolen away, lovely playmate of the invincible cry.

A dancer first who suddenly paused, her body stilled
by hesitation as if one cast her youthfulness in bronze;
mourning and listening –. Then, from powers on high,
music fell into her altered heart.

The illness was near. Already seized by the shadows,
her blood pulsed, darkened, and yet, as if momentarily suspect,
it rushed forth into its natural Spring.

Interrupted again and again by darkness and falling,
it shone of the earth. Until after terrible throbbing
it stepped inconsolably through the open gate.

26

Du aber, Göttlicher, du, bis zuletzt noch Ertöner,
da ihn der Schwarm der verschmähten Mänaden befiel,
hast ihr Geschrei übertönt mit Ordnung, du Schöner,
aus den Zerstörenden stieg dein erbauendes Spiel.

Keine war da, daß sie Haupt dir und Leier zerstör.
Wie sie auch rangen und rasten, und alle die scharfen
Steine, die sie nach deinem Herzen warfen,
wurden zu Sanftem an dir und begabt mit Gehör.

Schließlich zerschlugen sie dich, von der Rache gehetzt,
während dein Klang noch in Löwen und Felsen verweilte
und in den Bäumen und Vögeln. Dort singst du noch jetzt.

O du verlorener Gott! Du unendliche Spur!
Nur weil dich reißend zuletzt die Feindschaft verteilte,
sind wir die Hörenden jetzt und ein Mund der Natur.

26

But you, divine one, you, sounding forth to the very end
when overcome by the swarm of scorned maenads,
you, beautiful one, drowned out their cries with order
and from the ravagers your uplifting play arose.

No one of them could destroy your head and lyre.
How ever they wrestled and raced, and all the sharp
stones they hurled at your heart,
it all softened with you, endowed now with hearing.

Ultimately, they shattered you, harried by vengeance,
while the sound of your song lingered on in lions and rocks,
in the trees and among the birds. You're singing there even now.

O you lost god! You unending trace!
Only because this enmity in the end scattered you in rage
are we now the ones who hear and are a mouth of nature.

SECOND PART

1

Atmen, du unsichtbares Gedicht!
Immerfort um das eigne
Sein rein eingetauschter Weltraum. Gegengewicht,
in dem ich mich rhythmisch ereigne.

Einzige Welle, deren
allmähliches Meer ich bin;
sparsamstes du von allen möglichen Meeren, –
Raumgewinn.

Wieviele von diesen Stellen der Räume waren schon
innen in mir. Manche Winde
sind wie mein Sohn.

Erkennst du mich, Luft, du, voll noch einst meiniger Orte?
Du, einmal glatte Rinde,
Rundung und Blatt meiner Worte.

1

Breathing, you invisible poem!
Outer space purely exchanged
continually for its own being. Counterweight
within which I rhythmically transpire.

Solitary wave whose
gradual sea I am;
most frugal you of all possible seas, –
gained-space.

How many of these places, with all their rooms, were already
inside of me. Many winds
are like my son.

Do you know me, air, still filled as you are with places once mine?
You, rind once smooth,
curve and leaf of my words.

2

So wie dem Meister manchmal das eilig
nähere Blatt den *wirklichen* Strich
abnimmt: so nehmen oft Spiegel das heilig
einzige Lächeln der Mädchen in sich,

wenn sie den Morgen erproben, allein, –
oder im Glanze der dienenden Lichter.
Und in das Atmen der echten Gesichter,
später, fällt nur ein Widerschein.

Was haben Augen einst ins umrußte
lange Verglühn der Kamine geschaut:
Blicke des Lebens, für immer verlorne.

Ach, der Erde, wer kennt die Verluste?
Nur, wer mit dennoch preisendem Laut
sänge das Herz, das ins Ganze geborne.

2

Just as the sheet that's close at hand sometimes
catches the master's *real* stroke,
so mirrors often take into themselves
the girls' uniquely sacred smile

when they take stock of the morning, alone, –
or in the gleam of assisting lights.
And, later, only a reflection falls
into the breathing of their true faces.

What did eyes once glimpse as they gazed
into the hearths' charred and slowly-fading glow:
glances of life, forever lost.

Ah, who knows the Earth's losses?
Only one who yet praises aloud,
who sings the heart born into the whole.

3

Spiegel: noch nie hat man wissend beschrieben,
was ihr in euerem Wesen seid.
Ihr, wie mit lauter Löchern von Sieben
erfüllten Zwischenräume der Zeit.

Ihr, noch des leeren Saales Verschwender –,
wenn es dämmert, wie Wälder weit . . .
Und der Lüster geht wie ein Sechzehn-Ender
durch eure Unbetretbarkeit.

Manchmal seid ihr voll Malerei.
Einige scheinen *in* euch gegangen –,
andere schicktet ihr scheu vorbei.

Aber die Schönste wird bleiben –, bis
drüben in ihre enthaltenen Wangen
eindrang der klare gelöste Narziß.

3

Mirrors: never before has one knowingly described
what you in your essence truly are.
You, like interstices of time
filled with the sieve's many holes.

You, still squanderers of the empty hall –,
when dusk falls as in vast forests . . .
And the streetlamp, like a sixteen-pointer, passes
through your impenetrability.

At times you're full of paintings.
Some seem to have entered *into* you –,
others you shyly sent away.

But the loveliest of them will remain –, until
the clear, relaxed reflection of Narcissus
found its way there, to their chaste cheeks.

4

O dieses ist das Tier, das es nicht giebt.
Sie wußtens nicht und habens jeden Falls
 – sein Wandeln, seine Haltung, seinen Hals,
bis in des stillen Blickes Licht – geliebt.

Zwar *war* es nicht. Doch weil sie's liebten, ward
ein reines Tier. Sie ließen immer Raum.
Und in dem Raume, klar und ausgespart,
erhob es leicht sein Haupt und brauchte kaum

zu sein. Sie nährten es mit keinem Korn,
nur immer mit der Möglichkeit, es sei.
Und die gab solche Stärke an das Tier,

daß es aus sich ein Stirnhorn trieb. Ein Horn.
Zu einer Jungfrau kam es weiß herbei –
und war im Silber-Spiegel und in ihr.

4

O this is the creature that doesn't exist.
They didn't know it – its motion,
its bearing, its neck, all the way to the light
of its quiet gaze – and yet they loved it.

Indeed, it *didn't* exist. But because they loved it, it became
a pure creature. They always left room for it.
And in that room, clear and emptied,
it raised its head easily and hardly needed

to be. They never fed it with grain
but always with the chance that it might yet be.
And this lent the creature such power

that it sprouted a horn on its forehead. A horn.
Being white, it came to a virgin –
and was in the silvered mirror and within her.

5

Blumenmuskel, der der Anemone
Wiesenmorgen nach und nach erschließt,
bis in ihren Schoß das polyphone
Licht der lauten Himmel sich ergießt,

in den stillen Blütenstern gespannter
Muskel des unendlichen Empfangs,
manchmal *so* von Fülle übermannter,
daß der Ruhewink des Untergangs

kaum vermag die weitzurückgeschnellten
Blätterränder dir zurückzugeben:
du, Entschluß und Kraft von *wie*viel Welten!

Wir, Gewaltsamen, wir währen länger.
Aber *wann*, in welchem aller Leben,
sind wir endlich offen und Empfänger?

5

Flower-muscle that opens, little by little,
the meadow-morning of the anemone
until the bright sky's polyphonous light
pours itself forth into her womb,

tensed muscle of unending welcome
poured into the quiet star-bloom,
at times *so* overpowered with abundance
that the sunset's silent gesture

can hardly return to you
the leaves' widely sprung-back edges:
you, resolve and power of *how* many worlds!

We, the violent ones, we endure longer.
But *when*, in which of all lives,
will we finally be open and receivers?

6

Rose, du thronende, denen im Altertume
warst du ein Kelch mit einfachem Rand.
Uns aber bist du die volle zahllose Blume,
der unerschöpfliche Gegenstand.

In deinem Reichtum scheinst du wie Kleidung um Kleidung
um einen Leib aus nichts als Glanz;
aber dein einzelnes Blatt ist zugleich die Vermeidung
und die Verleugnung jedes Gewands.

Seit Jahrhunderten ruft uns dein Duft
seine süßesten Namen herüber;
plötzlich liegt er wie Ruhm in der Luft.

Dennoch, wir wissen ihn nicht zu nennen, wir raten . . .
Und Erinnerung geht zu ihm über,
die wir von rufbaren Stunden erbaten.

6

Rose, you enthroning one, to those of Antiquity
you were a chalice with a simple rim.
But for *us* you are the full, countless flower,
the inexhaustible object.

With your riches you seem like garment upon garment
wrapped around a body, made of nothing but radiance;
but each single petal of yours is both the avoidance
and the denial of all attire.

For centuries your scent has called
out its sweetest names to us;
suddenly it drifts like glory in the air.

Yet we don't know what to call it, we guess . . .
And memory, which we implored
through the hours we called, crossed over to it.

7

Blumen, ihr schließlich den ordnenden Händen verwandte,
(Händen der Mädchen von einst und jetzt),
die auf dem Gartentisch oft von Kante zu Kante
lagen, ermattet und sanft verletzt,

wartend des Wassers, das sie noch einmal erhole
aus dem begonnenen Tod –, und nun
wieder erhobene zwischen die strömenden Pole
fühlender Finger, die wohlzutun

mehr noch vermögen, als ihr ahntet, ihr leichten,
wenn ihr euch wiederfandet im Krug,
langsam erkühlend und Warmes der Mädchen, wie Beichten,

von euch gebend, wie trübe ermüdende Sünden,
die das Gepflücktsein beging, als Bezug
wieder zu ihnen, die sich euch blühend verbünden.

7

Flowers, you who're finally akin to arranging hands,
(hands of girls, past and present),
you who often lay on the garden table
from edge to edge, drooping and lightly wounded,

waiting for water that could once more revive them
from the first signs of death –, and now
flowers, streaming poles, lifted again
by feeling fingers, able to do still more

good than you suspected, you gentle ones,
when you found yourselves again in the vase,
cooling slowly and giving off girls' warmth

like confessions, like gloomy wearying sins
committed by being plucked, connecting again
with those who, in blooming, are bound to you.

8

Wenige ihr, der einstigen Kindheit Gespielen
in den zerstreuten Gärten der Stadt:
wie wir uns fanden und uns zögernd gefielen
und, wie das Lamm mit dem redenden Blatt,

sprachen als Schweigende. Wenn wir uns einmal freuten,
keinem gehörte es. Wessen wars?
Und wie zergings unter allen den gehenden Leuten
und im Bangen des langen Jahrs.

Wagen umrollten uns fremd, vorübergezogen,
Häuser umstanden uns stark, aber unwahr, – und keines
kannte uns je. *Was* war wirklich im All?

Nichts. Nur die Bälle. Ihre herrlichen Bogen.
Auch nicht die Kinder . . . Aber manchmal trat eines,
ach ein vergehendes, unter den fallenden Ball.

(*In memoriam Egon von Rilke*)

8

Few you are, playmates of a bygone childhood
in the city's scattered gardens:
how we found each other and were hesitantly pleased
and, like the lamb with the talking scroll,

spoke as those who kept silent. When we were glad then
belonged to no one of us. Whose was it?
And how it dissolved among all the people walking by
and amid the fright of the long year.

Carriages, drawn past us, rolled strangely by,
and houses stood around us, strong but untrue – without a one
of them ever recognizing us. *What* was real in space?

Nothing. Only the balls. Their splendid arcs.
Not even the children . . . But sometimes one of them,
ah, one passing away, stepped out beneath the falling ball.

(*In memory of Egon von Rilke*)

9

Rühmt euch, ihr Richtenden, nicht der entbehrlichen Folter
und daß das Eisen nicht länger an Hälsen sperrt.
Keins ist gesteigert, kein Herz –, weil ein gewollter
Krampf der Milde euch zarter verzerrt.

Was es durch Zeiten bekam, das schenkt das Schafott
wieder zurück, wie Kinder ihr Spielzeug vom vorig
alten Geburtstag. Ins reine, ins hohe, ins torig
offene Herz träte er anders, der Gott

wirklicher Milde. Er käme gewaltig und griffe
strahlender um sich, wie Göttliche sind.
Mehr als ein Wind für die großen gesicherten Schiffe.

Weniger nicht, als die heimliche leise Gewahrung,
die uns im Innern schweigend gewinnt
wie ein still spielendes Kind aus unendlicher Paarung.

9

Don't boast, you who judge, of dispensing with torture
and that iron no longer shackles necks.
Nothing is improved, no heart –, because a wanted
spasm of clemency pulls on you more tenderly.

What it acquired through the ages the scaffold
returns like children do with a toy from a bygone
birthday of long ago. Into the pure, the exalted,
the gatelike open heart he would step differently,

this god of true clemency. He would come with power,
more radiant in his reach as it is with gods.
More than a wind for the great sturdy ships.

Nor less than the gentle, hidden recognition
that quietly wins us over within,
like a gentle child at play from an unbounded mating.

10

Alles Erworbne bedroht die Maschine, solange
sie sich erdreistet, im Geist, statt im Gehorchen, zu sein.
Daß nicht der herrlichen Hand schöneres Zögern mehr prange,
zu dem entschlossenern Bau schneidet sie steifer den Stein.

Nirgends bleibt sie zurück, daß wir ihr *ein* Mal entrönnen
und sie in stiller Fabrik ölend sich selber gehört.
Sie ist das Leben, – sie meint es am besten zu können,
die mit dem gleichen Entschluß ordnet und schafft und zerstört.

Aber noch ist uns das Dasein verzaubert; an hundert
Stellen ist es noch Ursprung. Ein Spielen von reinen
Kräften, die keiner berührt, der nicht kniet und bewundert.

Worte gehen noch zart am Unsäglichen aus . . .
Und die Musik, immer neu, aus den bebendsten Steinen,
baut im unbrauchbaren Raum ihr vergöttlichtes Haus.

10

The machine threatens all that has been gained whenever
it dares to exist in our spirit rather than simply obeying.
That the exquisite hand's lovelier hesitation would shine no more
it cuts the stone more sharply for the sturdier building.

Nowhere does it hold back so that we could escape it just *once*
and let it simply belong to itself, oiling and all, in the silent factory.
The machine is life, – it thinks it can do it best,
ordering and creating and destroying with the same resolve.

But life is still enchanted for us; in a hundred
places it still is a source. A playing of pure
powers that no one touches who does not kneel and marvel.

Words still go forth tenderly before the unsayable . . .
And music, ever new, builds of the most tremulous stones,
in an unusable space, its divinized house.

11

Manche, des Todes, entstand ruhig geordnete Regel,
weiterbezwingender Mensch, seit du im Jagen beharrst;
mehr doch als Falle und Netz, weiß ich dich, Streifen von Segel,
den man hinuntergehängt in den höhligen Karst.

Leise ließ man dich ein, als wärst du ein Zeichen,
Frieden zu feiern. Doch dann: rang dich am Rande der Knecht,
 – und aus den Höhlen, die Nacht warf eine Handvoll von bleichen
taumelnden Tauben ins Licht . . .
                              Aber auch *das* ist im Recht.

Fern von dem Schauenden sei jeglicher Hauch des Bedauerns,
nicht nur vom Jäger allein, der, was sich zeitig erweist,
wachsam und handelnd vollzieht.

Töten ist eine Gestalt unseres wandernden Trauerns . . .
Rein ist im heiteren Geist,
was an uns selber geschieht.

11

Many a calmly ordered rule concerning death came forth,
onward-conquering man, since you held forth on the hunt;
I know you as more than trap or net, strip of sail
that one hangs down into the cavernous karst.

Someone let you in quietly as if you were a signal
to celebrate peace. But then: a servant wrestled you at the rim,
 – and, from the caves, the night hurled a handful of pale
careening doves into the light . . .
                              But even *this* is in the right.

Let every whiff of regret be far from the onlooker
and not from the hunter alone who, as is quickly clear,
alertly carries out his work.

Killing is one form of our wandering sorrow . . .
What happens to us ourselves
is pure in a serene spirit.

12

Wolle die Wandlung. O sei für die Flamme begeistert,
drin sich ein Ding dir entzieht, das mit Verwandlungen prunkt;
jener entwerfende Geist, welcher das Irdische meistert,
liebt in dem Schwung der Figur nichts wie den wendenden Punkt.

Was sich ins Bleiben verschließt, schon *ists* das Erstarrte;
wähnt es sich sicher im Schutz des unscheinbaren Grau's?
Warte, ein Härtestes warnt aus der Ferne das Harte.
Wehe –: abwesender Hammer holt aus!

Wer sich als Quelle ergießt, den erkennt die Erkennung;
und sie führt ihn entzückt durch das heiter Geschaffne,
das mit Anfang oft schließt und mit Ende beginnt.

Jeder glückliche Raum ist Kind oder Enkel von Trennung,
den sie staunend durchgehn. Und die verwandelte Daphne
will, seit sie lorbeern fühlt, daß du dich wandelst in Wind.

1 2

Desire the change. O be enthralled with the flame
in which a thing withdraws from you that brims with transformations;
that shaping spirit which masters the earthly
loves in the figure's swing nothing as much as the turning point.

What closes itself in staying the course *is* already rigid;
does it think itself secure in the shelter of inconspicuous gray?
Wait, for the hardest warns what is hard from afar.
Woe –: an absent hammer is ready to strike!

Whoever pours themselves forth as a spring the knowing knows;
and it leads them with delight through this serene creation
that often ends with beginning and with ending begins.

Every glad space they wander through, marveling,
is a child or grandchild of parting. And the transformed Daphne,
since feeling laurel-like, wants you to change yourself into wind.

13

Sei allem Abschied voran, als wäre er hinter
dir, wie der Winter, der eben geht.
Denn unter Wintern ist einer so endlos Winter,
daß, überwinternd, dein Herz überhaupt übersteht.

Sei immer tot in Eurydike –, singender steige,
preisender steige zurück in den reinen Bezug.
Hier, unter Schwindenden, sei, im Reiche der Neige,
sei ein klingendes Glas, das sich im Klang schon zerschlug.

Sei – und wisse zugleich des Nicht-Seins Bedingung,
den unendlichen Grund deiner innigen Schwingung,
daß du sie völlig vollziehst dieses einzige Mal.

Zu dem gebrauchten sowohl, wie zum dumpfen und stummen
Vorrat der vollen Natur, den unsäglichen Summen,
zähle dich jubelnd hinzu und vernichte die Zahl.

13

Be ahead of all parting as if it were behind
you like the winter now passing.
For among winters there is one so endlessly winter
that in overwintering it your heart just survives.

Be ever dead in Eurydice –, and climb more singingly,
climb more praisingly back into pure relation.
Here, among vanishing ones, be, in the realm of what remains,
be a ringing glass that shattered in sounding forth.

Be – and at the same time know the condition of not-being,
the unending ground of your heartfelt stirring,
in order to complete it fully this one time.

To what has been used as to the dull and mute provisions
of nature in its entirety, to the unspeakable sum of all this,
add yourself, rejoicing, and erase the count.

14

Siehe die Blumen, diese dem Irdischen treuen,
denen wir Schicksal vom Rande des Schicksals leihn, –
aber wer weiß es! Wenn sie ihr Welken bereuen,
ist es an uns, ihre Reue zu sein.

Alles will schweben. Da gehn wir umher wie Beschwerer,
legen auf alles uns selbst, vom Gewichte entzückt;
o was sind wir den Dingen für zehrende Lehrer,
weil ihnen ewige Kindheit glückt.

Nähme sie einer ins innige Schlafen und schliefe
tief mit den Dingen –: o wie käme er leicht,
anders zum anderen Tag, aus der gemeinsamen Tiefe.

Oder er bliebe vielleicht; und sie blühten und priesen
ihn, den Bekehrten, der nun den Ihrigen gleicht,
allen den stillen Geschwistern im Winde der Wiesen.

14

Look at the flowers, faithful to what is earthly,
to whom we lend fate from fate's edge, –
but who knows this! When they come repenting of their wilting,
it falls to us to be their regret.

Everything wants to hover. We go about here as those who burden,
laying ourselves on it all, enthralled with weight;
o what ruinous teachers we are for things,
because eternal childhood succeeds in them.

If one could take them into heartfelt slumber and sleep
deeply with things –: o how lightly he'd emerge
from that shared depth, altered for another day.

Or perhaps he'd stay; and they'd bloom and praise
him, the convert who now resembles them,
all of them quiet siblings in the meadow's wind.

15

O Brunnen-Mund, du gebender, du Mund,
der unerschöpflich Eines, Reines, spricht, –
du, vor des Wassers fließendem Gesicht,
marmorne Maske. Und im Hintergrund

der Aquädukte Herkunft. Weither an
Gräbern vorbei, vom Hang des Apennins
tragen sie dir dein Sagen zu, das dann
am schwarzen Altern deines Kinns

vorüberfällt in das Gefäß davor.
Dies ist das schlafend hingelegte Ohr,
das Marmorohr, in das du immer sprichst.

Ein Ohr der Erde. Nur mit sich allein
redet sie also. Schiebt ein Krug sich ein,
so scheint es ihr, daß du sie unterbrichst.

15

O fountain-mouth, you giver, you mouth
that voices one pure thing, inexhaustibly –
you, marble mask, before the water's
flowing face. And in the background,

the aqueducts' origin. Passing by graves
from afar, from the Apennines' slopes
they bear your speaking to you, which then
falls past the black aging of your chin

into the basin that is before it.
This is the sleeping ear laid down,
the marble-ear into which you always speak.

An ear of the Earth. Only with herself
does she thus speak. If a jug inserts itself,
she feels that you are interrupting her.

16

Immer wieder von uns aufgerissen,
ist der Gott die Stelle, welche heilt.
Wir sind Scharfe, denn wir wollen wissen,
aber er ist heiter und verteilt.

Selbst die reine, die geweihte Spende
nimmt er anders nicht in seine Welt,
als indem er sich dem freien Ende
unbewegt entgegenstellt.

Nur der Tote trinkt
aus der hier von uns *gehörten* Quelle,
wenn der Gott ihm schweigend winkt, dem Toten.

Uns wird nur das Lärmen angeboten.
Und das Lamm erbittet seine Schelle
aus dem stilleren Instinkt.

16

Torn open again and again by us,
the god is the place that heals.
We're keen in wanting to know,
but Orpheus is serene and spread all about.

He doesn't take even the pure, the consecrated
offering into his world in any other way
than by standing unmoved
across from the open end.

Only the dead one drinks
from the source we *heard* here,
when the god nods silently to him, the deceased.

To *us*, making noise is all that is offered.
And the lamb asks for its bell
from a quieter instinct.

17

Wo, in welchen immer selig bewässerten Gärten, an welchen
Bäumen, aus welchen zärtlich entblätterten Blüten-Kelchen
reifen die fremdartigen Früchte der Tröstung? Diese
köstlichen, deren du eine vielleicht in der zertretenen Wiese

deiner Armut findest. Von einem zum anderen Male
wunderst du dich über die Größe der Frucht,
über ihr Heilsein, über die Sanftheit der Schale
und daß sie der Leichtsinn des Vogels dir nicht vorwegnahm und
      nicht die Eifersucht

unten des Wurms. Giebt es denn Bäume, von Engeln beflogen,
und von verborgenen langsamen Gärtnern so seltsam gezogen,
daß sie uns tragen, ohne uns zu gehören?

Haben wir niemals vermocht, wir Schatten und Schemen,
durch unser voreilig reifes und wieder welkes Benehmen
jener gelassenen Sommer Gleichmut zu stören?

17

Where, in which ever blissfully watered gardens, on what
trees, from which tenderly unleafed flower-cups
do the exotic fruits of consolation ripen? These
delicious ones, one of which you'll find, perhaps, in the trampled meadow

of your poverty. From time to time
you'll marvel at the size of the fruit,
at its wholeness, at the softness of its rind,
and that neither the bird's imprudence nor the jealousy of the worm below

didn't first deprive you of it. Are there, then, trees frequented by angels,
trees so oddly pruned by patient, hidden gardeners
that they bear for us without being ours?

Have we who are shades and shadows never once been able
to disturb that calm summer serenity
through behavior at once prematurely ripe and then again wilted?

18

Tänzerin: o du Verlegung
alles Vergehens in Gang: wie brachtest du's dar.
Und der Wirbel am Schluß, dieser Baum aus Bewegung,
nahm er nicht ganz in Besitz das erschwungene Jahr?

Blühte nicht, daß ihn dein Schwingen von vorhin umschwärme,
plötzlich sein Wipfel von Stille? Und über ihr,
war sie nicht Sonne, war sie nicht Sommer, die Wärme,
diese unzählige Wärme aus dir?

Aber er trug auch, er trug, dein Baum der Ekstase.
Sind sie nicht seine ruhigen Früchte: der Krug,
reifend gestreift, und die gereiftere Vase?

Und in den Bildern: ist nicht die Zeichnung geblieben,
die deiner Braue dunkler Zug
rasch an die Wandung der eigenen Wendung geschrieben?

18

Dancer: o you transposing
all that is passing into motion: how you brought this forth.
And the whirl at the end, this tree made of movement,
didn't it fully possess the hard-won year?

Didn't the treetop bloom from stillness so that your swaying
of a moment ago might swarm around it? And above her,
wasn't she sun, wasn't she summer, the warmth,
this immeasurable warmth of you?

But it also bore, it bore your tree of ecstasy.
Aren't these its quiet fruits: the jug,
touched with ripening, and the ever-riper vase?

And in the images: doesn't the drawing remain
that the dark stroke of your brow
sketched quickly on the wall of your own turning?

19

Irgendwo wohnt das Gold in der verwöhnenden Bank
und mit Tausenden tut es vertraulich. Doch jener
Blinde, der Bettler, ist selbst dem kupfernen Zehner,
wie ein verlorener Ort, wie das staubige Eck unterm Schrank.

In den Geschäften entlang ist das Geld wie zuhause
und verkleidet sich scheinbar in Seide, Nelken und Pelz.
Er, der Schweigende, steht in der Atempause
alles des wach oder schlafend atmenden Gelds.

O wie mag sie sich schließen bei Nacht, diese immer offene Hand.
Morgen holt sie das Schicksal wieder, und täglich
hält es sie hin: hell, elend, unendlich zerstörbar.

Daß doch einer, ein Schauender, endlich ihren langen Bestand
staunend begriffe und rühmte. Nur dem Aufsingenden säglich.
Nur dem Göttlichen hörbar.

19

Gold lives somewhere in the pampering bank,
on familiar terms with thousands. But that
blind man, the beggar, is even for the copper coin
like a lost place, like the dusty corner under a cupboard.

In shops along the way money feels at home
and dresses deceptively in silk, carnations, and fur.
He, the one keeping silent, stands in the breath-pause
of all this money, breathing whether awake or asleep.

O how it might close itself at night, this ever-open hand.
Tomorrow it seizes fate again, and daily
fate holds it forth: bright, miserable, unendingly destructible.

If only someone, beholding all this in astonishment, would finally
grasp and praise this long endurance. Utterable only for the singer.
Audible only for the god.

20

Zwischen den Sternen, wie weit; und doch, um wievieles noch weiter,
was man am Hiesigen lernt.
Einer, zum Beispiel, ein Kind . . . und ein Nächster, ein Zweiter –,
o wie unfaßlich entfernt.

Schicksal, es mißt uns vielleicht mit des Seienden Spanne,
daß es uns fremd erscheint;
denk, wieviel Spannen allein vom Mädchen zum Manne,
wenn es ihn meidet und meint.

Alles ist weit –, und nirgends schließt sich der Kreis.
Sieh in der Schüssel, auf heiter bereitetem Tische,
seltsam der Fische Gesicht.

Fische sind stumm . . ., meinte man einmal. Wer weiß?
Aber ist nicht am Ende ein Ort, wo man das, was der Fische
Sprache wäre, *ohne* sie spricht?

2 O

Amongst the stars, what distances; and yet how much more distant still
what one learns from the here-and-now.
One, for example, one child . . . and the next, a second –,
o how incomprehensibly remote.

Perhaps fate measures us with the span of being
so that it appears strange to us;
consider how many spans there are from the girl to the man
when she avoids and yet wants him.

Everything is distant –, and nowhere does the circle close.
Look in the bowl on the brightly set table,
how odd the fish's face seems.

Fish are mute . . ., one once thought. Who knows?
But isn't there finally a place where one speaks what the fish's
language would be *without* them?

21

Singe die Gärten, mein Herz, die du nicht kennst; wie in Glas
eingegossene Gärten, klar, unerreichbar.
Wasser und Rosen von Ispahan oder Schiras,
singe sie selig, preise sie, keinem vergleichbar.

Zeige, mein Herz, daß du sie niemals entbehrst.
Daß sie dich meinen, ihre reifenden Feigen.
Daß du mit ihren, zwischen den blühenden Zweigen
wie zum Gesicht gesteigerten Lüften verkehrst.

Meide den Irrtum, daß es Entbehrungen gebe
für den geschehnen Entschluß, diesen: zu sein!
Seidener Faden, kamst du hinein ins Gewebe.

Welchem der Bilder du auch im Innern geeint bist
(sei es selbst ein Moment aus dem Leben der Pein),
fühl, daß der ganze, der rühmliche Teppich gemeint ist.

21

Sing the gardens, my heart, that you don't know; like gardens
poured into glass, clear and unattainable.
Waters and roses of Isfahan or Shiraz:
sing them blissfully and praise them, each incomparable.

Show, my heart, that you can never be without them.
That their ripening figs have you in mind.
That you consort with their winds that rise
to your face among the blooming branches.

Avoid the mistaken notion that anything is lacking
in the decision you've made: to be!
Silken thread, you're woven into the weave.

Whatever image you're inwardly joined to,
(if only a moment in this anguished life),
feel that the whole, the praiseworthy carpet is meant.

22

O trotz Schicksal: die herrlichen Überflüsse
unseres Daseins, in Parken übergeschäumt, –
oder als steinerne Männer neben die Schlüsse
hoher Portale, unter Balkone gebäumt!

O die eherne Glocke, die ihre Keule
täglich wider den stumpfen Alltag hebt.
Oder die *eine*, in Karnak, die Säule, die Säule,
die fast ewige Tempel überlebt.

Heute stürzen die Überschüsse, dieselben,
nur noch als Eile vorbei, aus dem waagrechten gelben
Tag in die blendend mit Licht übertriebene Nacht.

Aber das Rasen zergeht und läßt keine Spuren.
Kurven des Flugs durch die Luft und die, die sie fuhren,
keine vielleicht ist umsonst. Doch nur wie gedacht.

2 2

O despite fate: the exquisite abundances
of our existence, foamed-over in parks, –
or as stone-men standing beside the capstones
of high portals, rising like trees beneath balconies!

O the iron bell that raises its clapper
daily against the blunt everyday life.
Or that *one*, in Karnak, that column, the one
that outlives the only seemingly eternal temples.

Today the excesses rush by, the same ones,
but only as hurry, from the level, yellow
day into the dazzlingly light-exaggerated night.

But the frenzy passes without leaving a trace.
Arcs of flight through the air and those that drove them,
perhaps none of these is futile. Though only as thought.

23

Rufe mich zu jener deiner Stunden,
die dir unaufhörlich widersteht:
flehend nah, wie das Gesicht von Hunden,
aber immer wieder weggedreht,

wenn du meinst, sie endlich zu erfassen.
So Entzognes ist am meisten dein.
Wir sind frei. Wir wurden dort entlassen,
wo wir meinten, erst begrüßt zu sein.

Bang verlangen wir nach einem Halte,
wir zu Jungen manchmal für das Alte
und zu alt für das, was niemals war.

Wir, gerecht nur, wo wir dennoch preisen,
weil wir, ach, der Ast sind und das Eisen
und das Süße reifender Gefahr.

23

Call me to that one hour of yours
that unceasingly resists you:
imploringly close as the face of dogs,
but turned away again and again

just when you think you've finally grasped it.
For what's withdrawn is most certainly yours.
We are free. We were sent away there
where we thought we'd been first welcomed.

Fearfully, we clamor after support,
we, too young at times for what's old
and too old for what never was.

We're only justified when we yet praise,
because we, alas, are the branch and the blade
and the sweetness of ripening danger.

24

O diese Lust, immer neu, aus gelockertem Lehm!
Niemand beinah hat den frühesten Wagern geholfen.
Städte entstanden trotzdem an beseligten Golfen,
Wasser und Öl füllten die Krüge trotzdem.

Götter, wir planen sie erst in erkühnten Entwürfen,
die uns das mürrische Schicksal wieder zerstört.
Aber sie sind die Unsterblichen. Sehet, wir dürfen
jenen erhorchen, der uns am Ende erhört.

Wir, ein Geschlecht durch Jahrtausende: Mütter und Väter,
immer erfüllter von dem künftigen Kind,
daß es uns einst, übersteigend, erschüttere, später.

Wir, wir unendlich Gewagten, was haben wir Zeit!
Und nur der schweigsame Tod, der weiß, was wir sind
und was er immer gewinnt, wenn er uns leiht.

24

O this desire, ever new, from out of loosened clay!
Hardly anyone helped the earliest riskers.
Despite this, cities arose on blissful bays,
and water and oil yet filled the jugs.

The gods: we devise them first in daring drafts
that sullen fate then destroys.
Yet they are the immortal ones. Look, we may
listen to the one who hears us in the end.

We: a lineage across millennia of mothers and fathers,
ever more fulfilled by the future child
that, transcending us, might later shake us.

We, we the endlessly risked, how much time we have!
And taciturn death alone knows what it is that we are
and what he always gains in lending us.

25

Schon, horch, hörst du der ersten Harken
Arbeit; wieder den menschlichen Takt
in der verhaltenen Stille der starken
Vorfrühlingserde. Unabgeschmackt

scheint dir das Kommende. Jenes so oft
dir schon Gekommene scheint dir zu kommen
wieder wie Neues. Immer erhofft,
nahmst du es niemals. Es hat dich genommen.

Selbst die Blätter durchwinterter Eichen
scheinen im Abend ein künftiges Braun.
Manchmal geben sich Lüfte ein Zeichen.

Schwarz sind die Sträucher. Doch Haufen von Dünger
lagern als satteres Schwarz in den Aun.
Jede Stunde, die hingeht, wird jünger.

25

Listen, you can already hear the work
of the first rakes, the human beat again
in the restrained stillness of the hard
earth of early Spring. What's coming

seems yet untasted to you. And what's already
come to you, so often before, now seems
to come again as something new. Though always expected,
you never once took it. It has taken you.

Even the leaves of overwintered oaks,
in the evening, seem a coming brown.
Now and then the winds signal each other.

Black are the bushes. Yet piles of dung
are stored as a more fulsome black on the fields.
Each hour that slips by grows younger.

26

Wie ergreift uns der Vogelschrei . . .
Irgend ein einmal erschaffenes Schreien.
Aber die Kinder schon, spielend im Freien,
schreien an wirklichen Schreien vorbei.

Schreien den Zufall. In Zwischenräume
dieses, des Weltraums, (in welchen der heile
Vogelschrei eingeht, wie Menschen in Träume –)
treiben sie ihre, des Kreischens, Keile.

Wehe, wo sind wir? Immer noch freier,
wie die losgerissenen Drachen
jagen wir halbhoch, mit Rändern von Lachen,

windig zerfetzten. – Ordne die Schreier,
singender Gott! daß sie rauschend erwachen,
tragend als Strömung das Haupt und die Leier.

26

How bird-cry moves us . . .
Some particular once-made cry.
But even the children, playing outside,
cry out past real cries.

Cry chance. Into interstices
of this, of outer space (into which the whole
bird-cry enters like people in dreams –),
they drive their wedges of screeching.

Alas, where are we? Always yet freer,
we chase about in midair
like kites torn loose with fringes of laughter,

tattered by the wind. – Bring order to those who cry out,
singing god! that they might, roaring, awake,
bearing as flow both head and lyre.

27

Giebt es wirklich die Zeit, die zerstörende?
Wann, auf dem ruhenden Berg, zerbricht sie die Burg?
Dieses Herz, das unendlich den Göttern gehörende,
wann vergewaltigts der Demiurg?

Sind wir wirklich so ängstlich Zerbrechliche,
wie das Schicksal uns wahr machen will?
Ist die Kindheit, die tiefe, versprechliche,
in den Wurzeln – später – still?

Ach, das Gespenst des Vergänglichen,
durch den arglos Empfänglichen
geht es, als wär es ein Rauch.

Als die, die wir sind, als die Treibenden,
gelten wir doch bei bleibenden
Kräften als göttlicher Brauch.

27

Does time, the destroyer, truly exist?
When will it shatter the castle on the resting mountain?
This heart that belongs unendingly to the gods,
when will the demiurge overpower it?

Are we really, then, as fearfully fragile
as fate wants to make come true for us?
Is childhood, so deep, so promising
in the roots – later on – calm?

Alas, the specter of transience
passes through the guilelessly receptive one
as if it were smoke.

As those that we are, as achievers,
we're counted among abiding
powers as divine tradition.

28

O komm und geh. Du, fast noch Kind, ergänze
für einen Augenblick die Tanzfigur
zum reinem Sternbild einer jener Tänze,
darin wir die dumpf ordnende Natur

vergänglich übertreffen. Denn sie regte
sich völlig hörend nur, da Orpheus sang.
Du warst noch die von damals her Bewegte
und leicht befremdet, wenn ein Baum sich lang

besann, mit dir nach dem Gehör zu gehn.
Du wußtest noch die Stelle, wo die Leier
sich tönend hob –; die unerhörte Mitte.

Für sie versuchtest du die schönen Schritte
und hofftest, einmal zu der heilen Feier
des Freundes Gang und Antlitz hinzudrehn.

28

O come and go. You, almost still yet a child, extend
the dance-figure for an instant,
in a pure constellation, one of those dances
within which we momentarily surpass

nature, muffled in its ordering. For it roused itself
into full hearing only when Orpheus sang.
You were still the one moved from that time,
and a bit disconcerted, when a tree patiently

pondered following you by listening.
You knew the place still where the lyre
raised itself, sounding –; the extraordinary center.

For this you practiced these lovely steps
and hoped, someday, to turn your friend's gait and gaze
toward the unbroken celebration.

29

Stiller Freund der vielen Fernen, fühle,
wie dein Atem noch den Raum vermehrt.
Im Gebälk der finstern Glockenstühle
laß dich läuten. Das, was an dir zehrt,

wird ein Starkes über dieser Nahrung.
Geh in der Verwandlung aus und ein.
Was ist deine leidendste Erfahrung?
Ist dir Trinken bitter, werde Wein.

Sei in dieser Nacht aus Übermaß
Zauberkraft am Kreuzweg deiner Sinne,
ihrer seltsamen Begegnung Sinn.

Und wenn dich das Irdische vergaß,
zu der stillen Erde sag: Ich rinne.
Zu dem raschen Wasser sprich: Ich bin.

29

Quiet friend of the many distances, feel
how your breath expands the room.
Let yourself ring out among the rafters
of dark belfries. That which depletes you

will become a strength through this nourishing.
Go out and in again in transformation.
What's your deepest experience of suffering?
If drinking is bitter to you, become wine.

In the vastness of this night, be
a magic-power at the crossroad of your senses,
the meaning of their strange encounter.

And if the earthly has forgotten you,
say to the quiet Earth: I flow.
To the rushing water speak: I am.

DUINO
ELEGIES

FROM THE PROPERTY
OF PRINCESS MARIE VON THURN UND TAXIS-HOHENLOHE

DUINESER
ELEGIEN

AUS DEM BESITZ
DER FÜRSTIN MARIE VON THURN UND TAXIS-HOHENLOHE

❋

1912 – 1922
INSEL VERLAG, 1923

DIE ACHTE ELEGIE

Rudolf Kassner zugeeignet

Mit allen Augen sieht die Kreatur
das Offene. Nur unsre Augen sind
wie umgekehrt und ganz um sie gestellt
als Fallen, rings um ihren freien Ausgang.
Was draußen *ist*, wir wissens aus des Tiers
Antlitz allein; denn schon das frühe Kind
wenden wir um und zwingens, daß es rückwärts
Gestaltung sehe, nicht das Offne, das
im Tiergesicht so tief ist. Frei von Tod.
Ihn sehen wir allein; das freie Tier
hat seinen Untergang stets hinter sich
und vor sich Gott, und wenn es geht, so gehts
in Ewigkeit, so wie die Brunnen gehen.
   Wir haben nie, nicht einen einzigen Tag,
den reinen Raum vor uns, in den die Blumen
unendlich aufgehn. Immer ist es Welt
und niemals Nirgends ohne Nicht: das Reine,
Unüberwachte, das man atmet und
unendlich *weiß* und nicht begehrt. Als Kind
verliert sich eins im Stilln an dies und wird
gerüttelt. Oder jener stirbt und ists.
Denn nah am Tod sieht man den Tod nicht mehr
und starrt *hinaus*, vielleicht mit großem Tierblick.
Liebende, wäre nicht der andre, der
die Sicht verstellt, sind nah daran und staunen...
Wie aus Versehn ist ihnen aufgetan
hinter dem andern... Aber über ihn
kommt keiner fort, und wieder wird ihm Welt.
Der Schöpfung immer zugewendet, sehn
wir nur auf ihr die Spiegelung des Frein,
von uns verdunkelt. Oder daß ein Tier,
ein stummes, aufschaut, ruhig durch uns durch.

THE EIGHTH ELEGY

For Rudolf Kassner

With all its eyes the creature sees
the Open. Our eyes alone seem to be
reversed, set all around it
like traps encircling their free exit.
What *is* outside we come to know only
from the animal's face; for we already turn
the young child around so that it looks
backwards at things, and not into the Open, which
is so deep in the animal's face. Free of death.
Death is all we see; but the free animal
has its demise always behind it
and God ahead, and when it moves, it moves
in eternity just as fountains move.

    We never, not even for a single day, have
that pure space before us in which flowers
open without ceasing. Always it's world
and never Nowhere without No: the pure
and unobserved, which one breathes and
knows unceasingly, without craving. As a child
one loses oneself in the stillness of this until
shaken. Or that until one dies and *is* this.
For near to death one sees it no more
and stares *outwardly*, perhaps with an animal's great gaze.
Lovers, if it weren't for the other who blocks the view,
are near to this and marvel . . .
It's opened to them behind the other,
as if by mistake . . . But beyond him
no one comes forth, and it becomes world for him again.
Always turned toward creation, we see
only there the mirroring of what is free,
which we darken. Or an animal,
a mute one, looks up quietly and sees through us entirely.

Dieses heißt Schicksal: gegenüber sein
und nichts als das und immer gegenüber.

Wäre Bewußtheit unsrer Art in dem
sicheren Tier, das uns entgegenzieht
in anderer Richtung –, riß es uns herum
mit seinem Wandel. Doch sein Sein ist ihm
unendlich, ungefaßt und ohne Blick
auf seinen Zustand, rein, so wie sein Ausblick.
Und wo wir Zukunft sehn, dort sieht es Alles
und sich in Allem und geheilt für immer.

Und doch ist in dem wachsam warmen Tier
Gewicht und Sorge einer großen Schwermut.
Denn ihm auch haftet immer an, was uns
oft überwältigt, – die Erinnerung,
als sei schon einmal das, wonach man drängt,
näher gewesen, treuer und sein Anschluß
unendlich zärtlich. Hier ist alles Abstand,
und dort wars Atem. Nach der ersten Heimat
ist ihm die zweite zwitterig und windig.
    O Seligkeit der *kleinen* Kreatur,
die immer *bleibt* im Schoße, der sie austrug;
o Glück der Mücke, die noch *innen* hüpft,
selbst wenn sie Hochzeit hat: denn Schoß ist Alles.
Und sieh die halbe Sicherheit des Vogels,
der beinah beides weiß aus seinem Ursprung,
als wär er eine Seele der Etrusker,
aus einem Toten, den ein Raum empfing,
doch mit der ruhenden Figur als Deckel.
Und wie bestürzt ist eins, das fliegen muß
und stammt aus einem Schoß. Wie vor sich selbst
erschreckt, durchzuckts die Luft, wie wenn ein Sprung
durch eine Tasse geht. So reißt die Spur
der Fledermaus durchs Porzellan des Abends.

This is fate: to find oneself over against
and nothing but this and ever over against.

If our sort of consciousness existed
in the self-assured animal that moves toward us
in another direction –, it would tear us up
with its change. Yet it experiences its life
as unending, ungrasped, and without a sense
of its condition, pure as is its gaze.
And where we see future, it sees everything
and itself in everything and forever healed.

And yet this animal, alert and warm,
has the burden and worry of a great melancholy.
Because that which often overwhelms us
always clings to it as well, – the memory
that what one presses after had once been
closer and more faithful, its connection
unceasingly tender. Here, everything is distance;
there, it was breath. After the first homeland
the second is ambiguous and doubtful.
    O bliss of the *small* creature
that always *remains* in the womb that carried it;
o joy of the gnat that still hops about *within*,
even at its wedding: for womb is everything.
And see the half-assurance of the bird
that almost knows both from its beginnings,
as if it were an Etruscan's soul,
one deceased and placed in a chamber
with a carved figure resting on its lid.
And how dismayed is the one who must fly,
though coming forth from a womb. As if frightened of itself,
it flashes through the air like a crack that runs
through a cup. Just so, the bat's trail tears
through the porcelain of evening.

Und wir: Zuschauer, immer, überall,
dem allen zugewandt und nie hinaus!
Uns überfüllts. Wir ordnens. Es zerfällt.
Wir ordnens wieder und zerfallen selbst.

Wer hat uns also umgedreht, daß wir,
was wir auch tun, in jener Haltung sind
von einem, welcher fortgeht? Wie er auf
dem letzten Hügel, der ihm ganz sein Tal
noch einmal zeigt, sich wendet, anhält, weilt –,
so leben wir und nehmen immer Abschied.

And we: spectators always, everywhere,
turned toward it all and never looking out!
Everything overfills us. We put it in order. It falls apart.
We order it again and fall apart ourselves.

Who, then, has turned us around so that,
whatever we do, we have the posture
of one departing? Like one standing
the last hill that shows him his valley
once more in its entirety, who turns, pauses, lingers –,
thus we live, always taking our leave.

Warum, wenn es angeht, also die Frist des Daseins
hinzubringen, als Lorbeer, ein wenig dunkler als alles
andere Grün, mit kleinen Wellen an jedem
Blattrand (wie eines Windes Lächeln) –: warum dann
Menschliches müssen – und, Schicksal vermeidend,
sich sehnen nach Schicksal? . . .

              Oh, *nicht*, weil Glück *ist*,
dieser voreilige Vorteil eines nahen Verlusts.
Nicht aus Neugier, oder zur Übung des Herzens,
das auch im Lorbeer *wäre* . . . . .

Aber weil Hiersein viel ist, und weil uns scheinbar
alles das Hiesige braucht, dieses Schwindende, das
seltsam uns angeht. Uns, die Schwindendsten. *Ein* Mal
jedes, nur *ein* Mal. *Ein* Mal und nichtmehr. Und wir auch
ein Mal. Nie wieder. Aber dieses
ein Mal gewesen zu sein, wenn auch nur *ein* Mal:
irdisch gewesen zu sein, scheint nicht widerrufbar.

Und so drängen wir uns und wollen es leisten,
wollens enthalten in unsern einfachen Händen,
im überfüllteren Blick und im sprachlosen Herzen.
Wollen es werden. – Wem es geben? Am liebsten
alles behalten für immer . . . Ach, in den andern Bezug,
wehe, was nimmt man hinüber? Nicht das Anschaun, das hier
langsam erlernte, und kein hier Ereignetes. Keins.
Also die Schmerzen. Also vor allem das Schwersein,
also der Liebe lange Erfahrung, – also
lauter Unsägliches. Aber später,
unter den Sternen, was solls: *die* sind *besser* unsäglich.
Bringt doch der Wanderer auch vom Hange des Bergrands
nicht eine Hand voll Erde ins Tal, die Allen unsägliche, sondern

Why, when it is possible to while away
the span of existence as the laurel, a bit darker than all
other greens, with little waves on each
leaf-edge (like the smile of a breeze) –: why, then,
is humanness necessary – and, evading fate,
yearn for it? . . .

                          Oh, *not* because happiness *exists*,
this hasty gain of an imminent loss.
Not out of curiosity, or to exercise the heart,
as could also *be* for the laurel . . . . .

But because being-here matters so much, and because
all that is here-and-now seemingly needs us, this fleetingness that
strangely concerns us. Us, the most fleeting of all. *Once*
for each, only once. *Once* and not again. And we also
once. Never again. But to have been
this *once*, even if only *once*:
to have been *earthly*, this seems irrevocable.

And so we press on and want to achieve it,
want to hold it in our simple hands,
in our oversaturated vision and speechless heart.
Want to become it. Give it to whom? Preferably
hold onto all of it forever . . . Ah, what can one take over,
alas, into that other relation? Not the looking that's learned
so slowly here, and not what's happened here. Nothing of it.
Well, the pain. Well, above all, the difficulties,
well, the long experience of love, – which is to say,
nothing but the unsayable. But later,
among the stars, what then? *These* are *better* unsayable.
The wanderer doesn't take a handful of earth down to the valley, not even
from the slope at the mountain's edge, because this is unsayable to all,

ein erworbenes Wort, reines, den gelben und blaun
Enzian. Sind wir vielleicht *hier*, um zu sagen: Haus,
Brücke, Brunnen, Tor, Krug, Obstbaum, Fenster, –
höchstens: Säule, Turm . . . . aber zu *sagen*, verstehs,
oh zu sagen *so*, wie selber die Dinge niemals
innig meinten zu sein. Ist nicht die heimliche List
dieser verschwiegenen Erde, wenn sie die Liebenden drängt,
daß sich in ihrem Gefühl jedes und jedes entzückt?
Schwelle: was ists für zwei
Liebende, daß sie die eigne ältere Schwelle der Tür
ein wenig verbrauchen, auch sie, nach den vielen vorher
und vor den Künftigen . . . ., leicht.

Hier ist des *Säglichen* Zeit, *hier* seine Heimat.
Sprich und bekenn. Mehr als je
fallen die Dinge dahin, die erlebbaren, denn,
was sie verdrängend ersetzt, ist ein Tun ohne Bild.
Tun unter Krusten, die willig zerspringen, sobald
innen das Handeln entwächst und sich anders begrenzt.
Zwischen den Hämmern besteht
unser Herz, wie die Zunge
zwischen den Zähnen, die doch,
dennoch, die preisende bleibt.

Preise dem Engel die Welt, nicht die unsägliche, *ihm*
kannst du nicht großtun mit herrlich Erfühltem; im Weltall,
wo er fühlender fühlt, bist du ein Neuling. Drum zeig
ihm das Einfache, das, von Geschlecht zu Geschlechtern gestaltet,
als ein Unsriges lebt, neben der Hand und im Blick.
Sag ihm die Dinge. Er wird staunender stehn; wie du standest
bei dem Seiler in Rom, oder beim Töpfer am Nil.
Zeig ihm, wie glücklich ein Ding sein kann, wie schuldlos und unser,
wie selbst das klagende Leid rein zur Gestalt sich entschließt,
dient als ein Ding, oder stirbt in ein Ding –, und jenseits
selig der Geige entgeht. – Und diese, von Hingang
lebenden Dinge verstehn, daß du sie rühmst; vergänglich,
traun sie ein Rettendes uns, den Vergänglichsten, zu.

but rather brings an acquired and pure word, the yellow and blue
gentian. Perhaps we're *here* to say: house,
bridge, fountain, gate, jug, fruit tree, window, –
at best: column, tower . . . . But to *say*, you know,
oh, to say it just *so* thus as the things themselves could never
deeply mean to be. Isn't the secret ruse
of this reticent Earth, when it urges lovers on,
that this thing and that might delight in their feeling?
Threshold: what is it for two
lovers that they wear down the familiar threshold of their own door
a little more, and do this after the many who came before them
and before those yet to come . . ., gently.

Here is the time of the *sayable, here* its home.
Speak and bear witness. More than ever,
things that can be experienced fall apart, and
what forcibly replaces them is an imageless doing.
A doing beneath crusts that willingly shatter as soon as
this acting outgrows them inwardly and seeks new boundaries.
Our heart endures between
the hammers like the tongue
between our teeth, that in spite of this
yet praises.

Praise the world to the angel, not what is unsayable, for you
can't impress *him* with what's gloriously felt; in the universe
where he feels more acutely, you're a novice. So show
him some simple thing near to hand and within view,
shaped from generation to generation, that lives as one of ours.
Speak to him of things. He'll stand more amazed; as you
once stood by the roper in Rome or by the potter along the Nile.
Show him how happy a thing can be, how innocent and ours,
how even a lamenting sorrow resolves itself into a pure form,
serves as a thing or dies in a thing –, and blissfully escapes
beyond the violin. – And these things
that live by departing understand that you praise them; in their transience
they trust that we, the most transient of all, can save them.

Wollen, wir sollen sie ganz im unsichtbarn Herzen verwandeln
in – o unendlich – in uns! Wer wir am Ende auch seien.

Erde, ist es nicht dies, was du willst: *unsichtbar*
in uns erstehn? – Ist es dein Traum nicht,
einmal unsichtbar zu sein? – Erde! unsichtbar!
Was, wenn Verwandlung nicht, ist dein drängender Auftrag?
Erde, du liebe, ich will. Oh glaub, es bedürfte
nicht deiner Frühlinge mehr, mich dir zu gewinnen –, *einer*,
ach, ein einziger ist schon dem Blute zu viel.
Namenlos bin ich zu dir entschlossen, von weit her.
Immer warst du im Recht, und dein heiliger Einfall
ist der vertrauliche Tod.

Siehe, ich lebe. Woraus? Weder Kindheit noch Zukunft
werden weniger . . . . . Überzähliges Dasein
entspringt mir im Herzen.

They want us to transform them entirely in our invisible heart
into – o, unceasingly – into us! Whoever we might finally be.

Earth, isn't it this that you long for: to rise *invisibly*
within us? – Isn't it your dream
to be invisible one day? – Earth! invisible!
What, if not transformation, is your pressing task?
Earth, you beloved, I want this. Oh, believe that
not one more of your springtimes is needed to win me over to you – *one*,
oh, a single one is already too much for my blood.
Namelessly I'm committed to you from afar.
You were always right, and your holy intention
is an intimate death.

Look: I'm alive. From what? Neither childhood nor future
will diminish . . . . . Immeasurable life
springs forth from my heart.

AFTERWORD:
"*WE* MAKE THE WORLD OUR OWN"

With words and gestures, little by little,
we make the world our own ... (I.16)

The creative life rarely follows a schedule. It generally has its own way with us, obeying a rhythm and logic beyond the reach of our control. This was surely the case with Rainer Maria Rilke and with his *Sonnets to Orpheus* which came to him unexpectedly: after "receiving" the first twenty-six of them from February 2 – 5, 1922, he turned his attention back to the *Duino Elegies*, hoping to complete them from drafts and fragments written in the previous decade but subsequently abandoned under pressure of the war and its unsettling aftermath. He all but completed them in the form they finally took in the week that followed, from February 7 – 14, when he was interrupted again— by a second "dictation," as he later described it—that brought twenty-nine more sonnets, both parts coming to comprise the final shape of the *Sonnets to Orpheus*.[26] That creative outburst of February 1922 stands as one of the most extraordinary accomplishments of Rilke's life as a writer.

While the *Elegies* and the *Sonnets* have little in common, at least in formal terms, Rilke was convinced that these works belonged together: "both [works] reveal the identity of dreadfulness and bliss," he insisted, "like two faces on the same divine body, or rather a single face that presents itself in this way or that depending on the distance or the perspective from which we perceive it."[27] He also suggested that these two poem-cycles "continually support each other—, and I see an unending grace in how the same breath filled the small, rust-colored sails of the *Sonnets* and the immense white sailing-cloths of the *Elegies*."[28] Both invite readers to embrace the presence of this life, fleeting as it is, "because / all that is here-and-now seemingly needs us."[29]

Each stands as Rilke's own response to the anxious questions he had posed in a letter written during the early years of the war: "How is it possible," he wondered, "to live when the constitutive elements of our lives are completely beyond our grasp? How is it possible to exist at all when we prove to be continually inadequate at love, uncertain in our decisions, and incapable of facing death?"[30] Such doubts have lost nothing of their urgency for readers in our day: though we live a century after Rilke completed these works, his voice continues to grow in its appeal to those who long to wonder, with him, about how to make sense of life in the face of the divisiveness rending our societies and the environmental perils facing the Earth.

✳ ✳ ✳

How are we to approach such poems, requiring as they do a kind of patient and slow reading that seems out of step with late-modern sensibilities and habits? Is there a place in an age like ours, driven by speed and increasingly hobbled by ever shorter attention-spans, for poems like the *Sonnets* that are luscious in voice yet demanding to grasp? And, if there is, how do we attune ourselves to poems that require our full and sustained attention? The challenge is high, but the rewards are just as enriching, for as the first English translator of these poems, J. B. Leishman, put it,

> I feel, in reading [these poems], that we have come round the spiral to another "dawn of consciousness," where language is in the making, and where myth and symbol must often supply the place of not yet thinkable thoughts. No other writer is so full of the future; no other gives us such thrilling intimations of that inheritance on whose threshold we are standing, and which our civilization may be about to enter, if it does not perish through its own destructive forces.[31]

These uncertainties, and the peril surrounding them, have only grown over the century since these poems first appeared, even though the political and social circumstances we face are decidedly different from those of Rilke's day.

The opening stanzas in one of the relatively few poems he wrote during the war years articulate his brooding angst:

Here I am, here I am, one wrested,

staggering.
Can I yet dare it? Can I throw myself?

There where I pressed on were
many of the capable ones. Now, where
even the slightest execute total power,
keeping silent in the face of mastery –:
Can I yet dare it? Can I throw myself?[32]

Anguishing lines like these, which Rilke wrote in 1917, mirror the inertia of those times, which many among us still feel in the face of an increasingly uncertain future. War and rumors of war, the acceleration of unbridled technologies, a growing disregard for human dignity: these concerns, which he faced in his day, loom large in ours as well. *Can we yet dare it?*

Only with that context in mind can we begin to grasp the tensions present in the *Sonnets*: on the one hand they invite us to live exuberantly, to "dance the orange" and "throw [the warmer landscape] forth from within [us], so that the ripe orange might shine / in [our] homeland's winds!" (I.15), while on the other they wonder, in a more somber tone, "But *when*, in which of all lives, / will we finally be open and receivers?" (II.5). Something evocative and far-reaching is at work here, addressing us in pressing if also unresolved ways given the inner conflicts that burden us, now a century removed from their publication. If the *Sonnets* reveal the widening fissures that were already breaking apart long-held traditions and weakening the social and cultural institutions of Europe in Rilke's day, they meet us at a point much further down that path. Is this Orphic call something more than nostalgia? And can we hear it as a prophetic voice in late-modern societies like ours given how much is at stake in the transitions we find ourselves facing?

In either case, these poems seek to draw us beyond skepticism or resignation. His voice throughout these poems senses our anxieties, but precisely on this point he pivots to insist that "our entire existence, [with] the soarings and stumblings of our love" prepare us to engage this life since, as he put it in one of the last of these sonnets, "each hour that slips by grows younger" (II.25). He goes further to suggest that we are to be "transformers of the Earth," and, as if sensing that this might sound like a hollow platitude, he adds that the *Sonnets* unveil the "particularities" of that calling.[33] *We can dare this.*

The lyric voice Rilke establishes throughout the *Sonnets* carries an urgency shaped by a bold mix of determination and tenderness, as if he knows how much is at stake for his readers. He senses the way doubt had eroded the confidences of an earlier age, leaving us unsteadied and exposed; for this reason, perhaps, the temperament of these poems is marked by an abruptness of diction and a spaciousness of voice, an unlikely pairing that gives the sonnets a feeling of quiet velocity. And while Rilke can admit that "suffering has not been understood, / nor has love been learned, / and what distances us in death // is not unveiled", he goes on to voice his conviction, at the poem's close, that "only the song, over the land, / hallows and celebrates" (I.19). This bold claim is one we might not have expected to hear, and yet we long for it in the shadows of the fears and doubts that assail us.

Rilke's use of the imperative voice throughout the *Sonnets* directs this urgency toward the small things in life, inviting us to embrace the ordinary things around us simply because they *are* and not because of any meaning they might convey. Our work is to open ourselves to "being-here" [*Hiersein*], as he put it in the Ninth Elegy, learning to indwell our lives in ways that lead us into "the open end" they convey (II.16). The *Sonnets* expand upon this theme which is at the heart of that Elegy, reminding us that we are always alive only in the present, and thus encouraging us to embrace our life in all its "fleeting-ness" as belonging to "the Whole."

✳ ✳ ✳

As I have lived with these sonnets over the years, I have continually encountered them in different ways as if they were shape-shifting before me. Or perhaps I myself was changing in their presence. Again and again, phrases, images, even single words I'd either overlooked or underread have suddenly jolted something awake within me, bringing things forth from deep in the unconscious in moments of startling awareness. That said, these sonnets are not made for easy reading. They resist love at first sight, calling for a more patient courtship. One should not expect much from an initial reading; they call out to be read over and over again until one begins to become familiar with their startling idiosyncrasies and accustomed to their intractable strangeness.

The most effective journey into the intricacies of these sonnets calls for a slow entrance and repeated visits. Only such persistence enables us to sense, "little by little," a deepening resonance with their "words and gestures." As this happens, as they reveal themselves *to* us and *in* us over time, we begin to sense an acoustic resonance that leads us to an experience deeper than comprehension. For as Rilke reminded us, poems "are not, as many people think, feelings (one has those early enough in life),—they are experiences."[34]

The kind of experience the *Sonnets* beckon us toward has much to do with the intermingling sense of strangeness and familiarity they unexpectedly convey, one that evokes at once both distance and intimacy within us. Even when lines and whole poems have come to dwell in my mind, they still startle me on occasion as new associations arise and unexpected discoveries present themselves. A certain disorientation, after all, is necessary for a reorientation to occur. The paradox of this tension of proximity and distance is part of the sonnets' allure. They seem caught in that same blend of anticipation and confusion one has when listening to a jazz improvisation: one hears the central theme coming forward and then receding, moving from one instrument to another, the music flowing with a logic often hidden from the audience—and often enough from the performers themselves. Our experience of that theme, however, thickens as we listen, becoming layered as variations deepen our apprehension of "the whole" through the unexpected flow of the music. Only as the piece comes to an end can we "hear" a totality we could not have imagined in any other way.

Here, as in the *Sonnets*, familiarity comes and goes, and unpredictability is the one constant as the piece evolves. Such a performance calls for our full attention, giving us the feeling that the entire piece might fall apart at any moment, and sometimes does, releasing us only at the close into a different silence—and a deeper sense of presence—than we knew at the start. In just this manner, these poems offer themselves not as a set musical score offering renditions of a set theme, but rather as fluid improvisations with all the spontaneity and startlement this brings. But just as surely with the sense of fulfillment that their "performance" leaves with us.

It may well be that Rilke's composition of the *Sonnets*—which became one of the defining contributions of modernist literature—reflects something of this, composed after all just as jazz music was emerging as a novel musical and cultural form in America and the West. What is certain is that these poems breathe through the energy of their music, a feature we hear in Rilke's own description of how poems "live":

> Even when music speaks, it still does not speak to us. The perfectly created work of art concerns us only *insofar* as it survives us. The

poem enters from the inside into language, from a dimension that is always turned away from us; it fills language wonderfully and wells up within it to its rim—but from that point on it is beyond reach. . . [Music] is almost like the air of high regions: we breathe it deeply into the lungs of our spirit, and it infuses a more expansive blood into our hidden circulation. Yet *how far* music reaches beyond us! Yet *how much* of that which it carries right through us we still fail to seize! Alas, we fail to seize it, alas, we lose it.[35]

How better to understand the power of the *Sonnets* than to experience the music that carries them—and us as their readers—not as a gesture toward some form of *transcendence* beyond us, but as a *transcending* energy we find *within* us as we as "reach" through language and finally "beyond" it, and thus beyond *ourselves* as well.

If song is what shapes these sonnets and improvisation the characteristic that lends them fluidity and momentum, there is much more to these poems than music alone. There is movement and even a hint of dance. Often enough, in part at least because of this, these poems both convey to us and evoke within us as readers an almost breathless feeling of delight. This has much to do with their restless tempo, reflecting Rilke's experience of having received them "almost simultaneously," as he later put it. The frequent em-dashes found in most of the sonnets and the ellipses included in seventeen of them suggest that he found himself reaching through words for something he sensed at and beyond the edges of language: "But the winds . . . but the spaces . . ." (I.4). In the flow of these winds, and the spaciousness he came to call "the Open," we find ourselves as readers joining this silent listening to the point that we begin to identify with the singing god to whom Rilke addressed these sonnets. Singing becomes a form of self-forgetfulness and a kind of unselfconscious way of belonging to "the Whole."

Orpheus came to stand as an example of transformation for Rilke, just as the *Sonnets*, as he once put it, remind us of our capacity to "seize these things and appearances [in our lives] with the most fervent comprehension and transform them. Transform them? Yes, for such is our task: to impress this fragile and transient Earth so sufferingly, so passionately upon our hearts that its essence shall rise again, invisibly, within us."[36] In one sense, Rilke's Orpheus stands in our place as a change-agent, the "singing god" whose song embraced life on "this fragile and transient Earth" for the sake of transformation. In another, this god invites us to voice that song in our own lives. Ours, then, is the work of "desiring" that change (II.12) and entering into it without turning away. *Can we dare it?*

The sonnets thus call us to engage life in its *becomingness*, refusing the temptation to seek an escape *beyond* it. As he put it in a letter written late in his life,

> Here, what is passing plunges into the depths of being. And thus, all expressions of what is near to us are not to be grasped merely as time-bound, but rather, and as far as this is possible for us, we are to transpose them into those superior meanings in which we participate. But *not in a Christian sense* (from which I distance myself with increasing passion), but in a purely earthly, profoundly earthly, blessedly earthly consciousness is it valid to bring all that we here observe and touch into a wider, into the widest horizon. Not into an otherworldliness [*jenseits*] whose shadows darken the Earth, but into a whole, into *the Whole*.[37]

These poems invite us into this "blessedly earthly consciousness," one that upholds "the depths of being" not *beyond* this life but in its "here-and-now-ness" (*das Hiesige*). Their voice celebrates an abundance that is ever present, a richness that life's impermanence and brokenness cannot erase: "O despite the exquisite abundances / of our existence . . ." (II.22). The same theme resounds in the closing lines of the Ninth Elegy: "Immeasurable life / springs forth from my heart."

The *Sonnets* follow this lead, inviting us to live into "the Whole" in terms of the particularities of this life. This is the insight Rilke was so keen on articulating in the *Elegies* and showing in the *Sonnets*. As he put it late in the Ninth Elegy:

> Earth, isn't it this that you long for: to rise *invisibly*
> within us? – Isn't it your dream
> to be invisible one day? – Earth! invisible!
> What if not transformation is your pressing task?
> Earth, you beloved, I will.

The will to "desire the change" (II.2), to want this transformation and risk embracing it fully, finds expression again and again in these sonnets. In poems like this, bursting with expressions of delight, Rilke joins the sense of this urgency to the experience of bliss: "O experience, sensation, joy –, immense!" (I.13). Rilke invokes Orpheus throughout these sonnets as the "singing god" who knew to celebrate life in its abundance at the heart of its changes.

Yet when he turns to Orpheus in the final poem of the First Part with an unexpected vocative cry, "O you lost god! You unending trace!" (I.26), we begin to sense that this singer is no longer present:

> O that he must fade away for you to grasp this!
> Even though he himself feared he would vanish.
> When his word exceeds this being-here,
>
> he's already there where you can't accompany him. (I.5)

Orpheus is already and always here in the singing, even when he is "lost" and has fallen silent: "Once and for all / it's Orpheus when there's singing. He comes and goes" (I.5). As heirs to his silence, we become those called to find him, not only in the song but through our own singing.

This is a crucial point in grasping the flow of these sonnets, for Rilke comes to imagine Orpheus as listening for *us*, as if awaiting *our* discovery that "song is Being" (*Gesang ist Dasein*), a phrase that might also be rendered "song is being-here," "song is existence," "song is presence," or simply "song is life." We inherit Orpheus' call to sing, and become Orphic messengers as we do, standing in the place where the singing god once stood as we learn to "make the world our own." Perhaps this is the reason Rilke presents Orpheus as the singer who has "come and gone," the "lost god" who has yet left behind an "unending trace" (I.26)—in the singing that continues. For he is the one who still listens for us along the margins of these sonnets, and just as his song once enchanted the "creatures of stillness," that song still builds "temples in [our] hearing."

❋ ❋ ❋

The theme of listening, at the heart of the first sonnet, comes to shape the poem-cycle in its entirety. What Rilke underscores here is the way that singing and listening form an indissoluble unity, a convergence that shapes the *Sonnets* from beginning to end. It also acquaints us with the distinctive melody of his voice, shaped in large measure by the sequence of images he unveils in the process. If this piece stands as a witness of praise to *Orpheus,* introducing this divine magician-singer of Antiquity who was "the first singer of holy songs and the founder of their mysteries," it also underscores the role of listening as the natural matrix of music.[38]

The opening lines of the first sonnet burst forth with a tumble of startling vocatives—"There a tree arose. O pure transcending! / O Orpheus is singing! O tall tree in the ear!"—and then turn immediately to the audience: "and everything kept still." Singing has little resonance without true listening, rooted as this is in the capacity of "keeping silent" (*schweigen*), to recall the resonant word Rilke uses here and repeatedly throughout these poems. Keeping silent, listening, and singing: these postures join us to Orpheus, and their resonance opens to us the energies of transformation.

In the Eighth Elegy in particular, Rilke envisioned animals as modeling for us what it is to live always listening, always availing themselves—as they do—of "the Open." Their attentiveness to "hereness" becomes a living witness for us, and as we silence ourselves to the point that we are able to listen to the "stillness"—to the point of hearing "the sound of silence"[39]—we find ourselves entering into the spaciousness of Orpheus' song:

> And there
> where a meager hut stood to receive them,
>
> a refuge made of darkest desires
> with an entrance whose doorjambs tremble, –
> you built temples for them in their hearing. (I.1)

Orpheus' "temples," of course, are not places. They point to a state of being, a quiet form of receptivity. Orpheus had not simply built external "temples" *for their hearing;* they were "built," rather, *through their listening.* This capacity is what creatures and living things instinctively know to do, a reminder—if we needed one, as we apparently do—that creatures seem to have less need of us than we do of them in order to survive, if not thrive, on this Earth.

✳ ✳ ✳

We grasp the intent of this conviction when we recall that while Rilke may have written these sonnets *to* Orpheus, he dedicated them to a young woman he had only met on several occasions, publishing them with the inscription "A grave-memorial for Vera Ouckama Knoop." Rilke had seen Vera dance as a young teenager when he visited Munich in 1914, and his daughter Ruth befriended her there in the years that followed. But Vera's desire to give her life to dance foundered with the onset of leukemia in the years that followed, the same illness, ironically, that would end Rilke's life several years later. As the disease began to paralyze her and she was no longer able to dance, she turned her artistic passions to music and drawing.

News of Vera's death, in December of 1919, first reached Rilke several years later, and his immediate response was to write a lengthy consolatory letter to her mother, Gertrud. A package from her arrived, in response, on New Year's Day, 1922, containing a copy of the journal Gertrud had kept as a chronicle of her daughter's illness during the last years of her life and her eventual death. There, he read her account of how

> . . .[t]his beautiful child, who had just begun to dance and had cre-
> ated a sensation among all who saw her, through whom the art of
> movement and transformation expressed so innately in her body
> and spirit passed,—told her mother unexpectedly that she could
> not and would not dance any more . . . (This happened as she
> entered puberty.) In the time still left to her, Vera took up music,
> and finally she only made drawings, as if the dance that now failed
> her came forth from her in ever quieter and more subtle forms.[40]

Rilke was so moved by this story of Vera's artistic transformation that he wrote a passionate letter to her grieving mother sometime in the weeks that followed. He voiced his sorrow, of course, but also expressed his admiration of her daughter's courage in transforming her creativity from one artistic mode into another: "You knew the place still where the lyre / raised itself sounding –; the extraordinary center." (II.28).

Rilke went on to voice his conviction that this metamorphosis expressed Vera's sense of belonging to what he had come to call simply "the Whole." Through the witness of her transformation in the face of illness and her eventual death, he came to see "how marvelous, how singular, how incomparable the human person is!" He saw in her creativity a resilience to embrace change, and in that process "there arose, when everything seemed to have been expended, suddenly—which otherwise could have been reached-for through a long being-(where?)-here [Da-(Wo?)-sein]—there arose an excess of light in the heart of this girl, and within her shone forth with unending radiance the unity of heaven and Earth." Rilke marveled at what he called "this oned oneness" (dieses einige Einssein) of hers, in the face of her suffering, and how she "opened her heart entirely" to

> the unity of this living and resilient world, this assent to life, this joyful, stirring sense of belonging to everything that is here, all the way to the end—alas, and surely not only to what is here?! No, (what she could not have known in the first attacks of this ending and departure!)—into the *Whole*, which is much more than what is here.[41]

He came to see Vera's "assent to life" as the crux of the transformation Orpheus gave voice to with his song, which in its own way joined the various parts of this world in a "oned oneness."

Vera's creative resilience, her embrace of change, is what brought her to "complete" the dance in new forms. What the poet had come to know of Orpheus he now attributed to her as well: "O, that [Orpheus] must fade away for you to grasp this!" (I.5). If Vera came to stand for Rilke as Orpheus for her capacity to transform life in the face of death, she also came to represent Eurydice, a reference that clarifies Rilke's otherwise enigmatic charge to "be ever dead in Eurydice" (II.13). Only in giving ourselves completely to the flow of change, in death as in life, only by singing in the face of death, do we come to know what art is about: "Singing God, how did you / so perfect her that she did not desire / first to awake? Look, she arose and slept." (I.2).

✳ ✳ ✳

In times like ours, when many feel unable to live with creativity and resilience in the face of what has been recently described as "an epidemic of loneliness and isolation,"[42] Rilke's *Sonnets* offer a useful grounding. They encourage us to persevere in "the soarings and stumblings of love"—of ourselves together with the creatures and things of this world. They seek to instill a confidence in how we might embrace the sufferings and joys of this life, all the way to our death, as part of "the Whole." They also invite us with an urgent persuasiveness to risk transformation in the "here-and-now" of our lives. As a writer drawn to what he often referred to as *Innigkeit*—an untranslatable word that could be rendered as "closeness," suggesting both intimacy and depth, intensity as well as warmth—Rilke signals his awareness of the unsettling pressures of loneliness, the anguishing malaise of modernity. But he knew that solitude was essential, providing us with the *Innigkeit* needed to discover how we belong to each other within "the Whole."

How we do this depends upon the courage and creativity by which we engage our life in its "here-ness" (*Hiersein*). One of the most startling of Rilke's Orphic invitations, in this regard, is his admonition to "dance the orange." From the earliest of these sonnets to the last we find them inviting us to embrace life with all its sensuousness: to "dance the savor of fruit you've tasted!" (I.15) and "savor" the fruits—"fullness of apple, banana and pear, / gooseberry" (I.13), affirming the sweet along with the bitter (gooseberries, after all!). Yet his voice summons us to discover the "pure tension" held in this dance, one arising from the mysterious bond of resistance and ease, "dreadfulness and bliss" we face in our lives. As we discover how the orange offers itself "deliciously" to us, Rilke reminds us that we come to "dance" the "warmer landscape" where this fruit grew, experiencing "the unity of this living and resilient world,"[43] as he imagined it:

> The warmer landscape,
> throw it forth from within you so that the ripe orange might shine
> in your homeland's winds! In its glowing it unveils
>
> fragrance upon fragrance. (I.15)

Rilke knows, too, that this does not come easily: the rind of the orange, with its stubborn bitterness, is part of what he calls us to "dance"; we must peel away the rind, unveiling as we do "fragrance upon fragrance." In opening ourselves to this "dance," we come to delight in the "intensifying sweetness" of the orange's juice. But he reminds us that the bitter rind is not simply something to discard; it belongs to this experience, and ours is the task of entering into relationships with it as well:

> Establish kinship

with the pure, resisting rind,
with the juice that fills the happy fruit! (I.15)

What is the gift of this "happy" fruit, this orange whose gift it is to delight? And who are we to risk dancing the orange? Such images, strange and delightful at once, invite us to immerse ourselves in the fullness of life, through such gestures of embodiment, discovering in the journey that we belong as an indispensable part to "the Whole." Indeed, in one of the late sonnets Rilke goes so far as to praise what we have not yet experienced, to delight in what may ultimately lie beyond our grasp but is always within reach of our imagination:

Sing the gardens, my heart, that you don't know; like gardens
poured into glass, clear and unattainable.
Waters and roses of Isfahan or Shiraz:
sing them blissfully and praise them, each incomparable. (II.21)

❋ ❋ ❋

Rilke sensed that our vocation as human beings was ultimately that of praising, in the midst of our losses—as Orpheus had done, and Vera after him. And as he felt himself doing in and through these sonnets:

Ah, who knows of the Earth's losses?
Only the one who yet praises aloud,
who sings the heart, born into the Whole. (II.2)

What a vivid image this is, pointing to the music Rilke invites us not simply to listen for, but to perform in our lives as we dare to join in this heartful singing, and thus find ourselves "born into the Whole."

Here as throughout the *Sonnets* Rilke voices the call to live in praise. Such a life, with its resonance and the resilience it brings, is a theme woven through the fabric of these poems. In a poem he inscribed in the book of a friend as a dedication, he put it this way:

Oh say, poet, what is it that you do?
– I praise.

But what of the deadly and monstrous,

how do you endure all this, how do you take it in?

    – I praise.

But the nameless, the anonymous,

how, despite it all, do you keep calling to them, poet?

    – I praise.

Where does it come from, your claim to be true

in every guise and in each mask?

    – I praise.

And that stillness and turbulence

know you like star and storm?

    – Because I praise.[44]

❋ ❋ ❋

These sonnets address what Rilke knew as our "innermost consciousness," the "wakefulness" within us that knows to embrace what he called the "eternal childhood" of all living things. In poem after poem, he celebrates the "common depth" (II.14) that lies within us and all things. He reminds us throughout the sonnets, as in the two late Elegies included here, that "being-here matters so much." These sonnets celebrate our "earthliness," urging us again and again to seize the one life we have, "*once* and . . . never again." This orientation grounds his call to "sing [our] heart," which is to say, to live praising in the face of the gains and losses that come to us. Indeed, the sonnet that opens with his call to "look at the flowers, faithful to the earthly" (II.14) invites us—as he put it in the Eighth Elegy—to open ourselves into that "pure space before us in which flowers open without ceasing"—and, in our own faithfulness to the earth, to find the world praising *us* as we become "converts":

> If [we] could take them into heartfelt slumber and sleep
> deeply with things –: o how lightly [we'd] emerge
> from that common depth, altered, to another day.
>
> Or perhaps [we'd] stay; and they'd bloom and praise
> [us], the converts who now resemble them,
> all of them quiet siblings in the meadow's wind. (II.14)

Here, Rilke wonders what might happen if *we* learned to live into "the Open," to celebrate the "common depth" (*die gemeinsame Tiefe*) we share with all that is, creatures and things and the Earth itself. It would be as if all that is "here" came to "bloom and praise" us as "converts"—to the point that we became "quiet siblings" with them "in the meadow's wind."

What an exquisite vision this is, inviting us to recover that inner spaciousness we once knew in childhood and find ourselves called to experience again in our adult years. And what a remarkable vision to imagine that the world to which we belong praises *us* when we enter into this transformation. Throughout the meanderings of this poem-cycle, Rilke's call to "desire [this] change" becomes the guiding leitmotif of the whole cycle. Through it, we discover within ourselves what he describes as the "shaping spirit" that "masters the earthly," loving as it does "in the figure's swing nothing as much as the turning point" (II.12).

Rilke knew that much depends on that "turning point," and the last of the *Sonnets* beckon us to embrace this possibility as both gift (*Gabe*) and charge (*Aufgabe*). These poems invite us to face with bravery what we can neither manage nor control—"O despite fate. . ."—and find there "the exquisite abundances / of our existence" (II.22). Throughout these poems Rilke holds to the conviction that we are creatures who have the capacity to open ourselves to those "exquisite abundances" as ones who belong—with all else—to "the Whole." In this recognition, we come to find our essential identity bound with all that is "earthly"—for, as he put it memorably in the Ninth Elegy, "to have been *earthly*, this seems irrevocable." In myriad ways, then, Rilke beckons us in the Sonnets to savor the "here-and-now-ness" of life for its inherent fullness, embracing all that it brings of delight and suffering. Ours is the call to "dance the orange," rind and all, living to praise in the face of the joys and sorrows that come our way.

❋ ❋ ❋

If the first of these sonnets opens with an address to Orpheus, that builder of "temples" for creatures "in their hearing" (I.1), they close in the final poem with what might be interpreted as Rilke's earth-directed, life-affirming credo. Here, he gives voice one last time to his call that we live into that sense of "the Open" as we "feel / how [our] breath expands the room." Here, we find him celebrating our capacity to face what depletes us, with courage and trust, finding "strength through this nourishing." Here, too, he reminds us that when our "drinking is bitter," it falls to us to "become wine." And here, without a trace of sentimentality or wishful thinking, he invites us to "go out and in again in transformation," discovering as we do the "exquisite abundances" of the "here-and-now" (*das Hiesige*).

This realization entices us to join Rilke in crying out, "o pure transcending!" (I.1), recognizing that the "outside" world is *within* us—"O tall tree in the ear!" (I.1), that outer and inner, here and beyond, then and now cohere in "the oned oneness" that Rilke knew as "the Whole." For this, too, is how "with words and gestures, *we* make the world our own." The final witness of Rilke's *Sonnets to Orpheus*, which are ultimately sonnets to *us*, affirms our vocation to "sing the heart, born into the Whole," and, as we do, to praise the gift of life, come what may:

> And if the earthly has forgotten you,
> say to the quiet Earth: I flow.
> To the rushing water speak: I am. (II.29)

ACKNOWLEDGMENTS

The emergence of this translation has been a project stretching over several decades, and I have benefited from the interest, support, and encouragement of many colleagues and friends along the way. This all began when I found myself, many years ago, experimenting with my own renditions in the attempt to avoid the pitfall—to my mind—that many modern English versions have fallen into: namely, the decision to soften the peculiarity of these poems by smoothing over their often-broken or heavily-twisted diction and choosing "sensible" words or pleasing phrases for those that native German readers would find strange and even jarring.[45]

My intention in doing so was to retain for English readers something of the startlement along with the delight that the sonnets evoke for those reading them in the poet's German. I felt strongly then, and feel even more strongly now, that the attempt to do this was and is true to Rilke's intent, and thus worth the risk to readers who might find such renditions initially strange if not confusing. It seemed to me that only such an approach could give expression to his intent in writing these sonnets as he did. With the harvest of those labors now in hand, I trust that readers will be able to discover this for themselves as they enter the strange and marvelous world of these poems.

I began work on a full translation during my years on the faculty of the Protestant University of Applied Sciences in Bochum, Germany. I am grateful to the university for granting me a sabbatical in 2018–2019 to devote myself to this work and for the generous support of a student assistantship that academic year and during the one that followed. It is with pleasure that I thank Lisa Borgschulte for admirably fulfilling that role; we ventured into these poems together with a steady mix of curiosity and fascination. I thank her for that early accompaniment and for the insights and thoughtful suggestions she shared at many points along the way.

I am also glad to thank Stephanie Dowrick for the many hours of conversation about Rilke's writings that have shaped my life over the many years since we first met. Those discussions contributed in important ways to my understanding of Rilke's work and have been equally significant for my grasp of the deep wellspring of experience from which these poems first arose and toward which they gesture: "Go out and in again in transformation" (II.29). This collaboration blossomed into a friendship for which I am immensely grateful. It has also led to various collaborations, among them our co-authoring of a forthcoming book, *You Are the Future: Living the Questions with Rainer Maria Rilke.* The writing of that book has been a labor of shared creativity and mutual discovery.

I have also gained much through the years from conversations about Rilke's poems with my spouse, Ute Molitor, a native German speaker and, with me, a lover of his writings. His *Sonnets* in particular have accompanied us across the span of our lives, leading to countless fruitful exchanges as we explored the eccentricities of Rilke's images and the intricacies of his peculiar diction. These are poems meant to be lingered over, as we have done, savoring their idiosyncratic beauty and "meanderings" amid the alluring puzzles of the imaginative world that they conjure. The *Sonnets* have often been enough at the heart of our conversations and musings, drawn as we both are by the magnetism of Rilke's strangely inventive diction and beguiling lyricism.

My work on Rilke has been shaped above all through my long friendship with Gotthard Fermor whom I first met when he was a faculty member at the Protestant University of Applied Sciences in Bochum, Germany. I eventually accepted a professorship at that university and taught there from 2012 until 2020; over the course of those years our shared passion for Rilke's poetry led to a collaboration, under his editorship, on a three-volume German edition of Rilke's *Book of Hours.*[46] As my work on this volume was nearing completion, Gotthard joined me for an intense "cross-reading" of these poems. We explored each of them slowly, line by line and often phrase by phrase in German, seeking to find felicitous ways to render their complex lyricism and often baffling diction into an English capable of rendering the distinctive and often eccentric voice they carry—or that carries them. What was particularly important in this collaboration was the effort, on the one hand, to maintain in the English versions something of the alluring strangeness of Rilke's German syntax, and, on the other, to keep alive what the poet himself described as the "radiant darkness" found in them.

In a more formal sense, I am glad to thank the editors of *91st Meridian*, the journal of the University of Iowa's International Writing Program, for publishing four early versions of these sonnets (I.1, I.3, I.22, and I.23) in 2015. I am particularly grateful to the program's director, Christopher Merrill, for his enthusiasm about this project in its early stages and ever since. Three of these sonnets (I.19, I.22, and II.21) also appeared in a collection of my own poems, *The Chance of Home* (Brewster, MA: Paraclete Press, 2018) and one of them (I.19) was published in 2009 in a limited letterpress edition by the Bow and Arrow Press of Cambridge, MA, commissioned by the Honorable Mark L. Wolf.

Finally, it is my privilege to thank Paul Cohen and Monkfish Book Publishing Company for bringing this book to print. I am particularly grateful to their literary editor Anne McGrath who took an immediate interest in this project and offered unswerving support and thoughtful advice from start to finish. Colin Rolfe shaped the book's design with an artist's eye and a master's hand, from the brilliant cover to every detail of its layout, and Dory Mayo tracked down a host of small details in her vigilance as copy editor. Every author knows the importance of such people; few are as fortunate as I have been to have a team this creative and responsive on my side.

NOTES FOR THE SONNETS

The italicized notes, below, are attributed to Rilke. These can be found, along with other brief explanatory comments, in the "Commentary" section of the *Werke. Kommentierte Ausgabe in vier Bänden,* vol. 2: *Gedichte 1910–1926,* ed. by Manfred Engel and Ulrich Fülleborn (Frankfurt am Main and Leipzig: Insel Verlag, 1996), 729–64; these are also found in the *Werkausgabe* of Rilke's *Sämtliche Werke,* vol. 2, ed. Rilke-Archiv (Frankfurt am Main: Insel Verlag, 1955), 772–73. Only two of these notes—to I.21 and II.22—were included when the poem-cycle was first published in 1923; the others, attributed to Rilke, were added by his publisher in later editions. All other notes are my own, offered as aids to readers who might be unfamiliar with some of the references found in these sonnets; they also include occasional cross-references to other sonnets in this collection, to the *Duino Elegies,* and to Rilke's letters and other poems, as pertinent.

I.1   Rilke's reliance on legends about Orpheus points primarily to Ovid's *Metamorphoses,* which he received in a French translation as a gift from "Merline" (Balladine Klossowska). For a discussion of these legends, see Ann Wroe, *Orpheus. The Song of Life* (London: Jonathan Cape, 2011). For a more detailed and technical discussion of Rilke's approach to Orpheus in the context of modernist (European) literature, see Charlie Louth, *Rilke: The Life of the Work* (Oxford: Oxford University Press, 2020), 455–63.

I.2   Rilke suggested in a letter of 1923 that two of the sonnets—the penultimate ones in each of the two parts (I.25 and II.28) refer directly to Vera Ouckama Knoop, though others—including this one—seem to have her in mind.

I.5   The image of the rose played a central role in Rilke's life, inspiring the inscription he asked to be placed on his tombstone, and while it would be anachronistic to read that inscription back into this poem, the thematic echo is clear enough:

> Rose, oh pure contradiction, desire
> to be no one's sleep beneath so many
> eyelids.

I.6 The willow has often served as an image of mourning. Earth-smoke refers to the herb, fumitory; together with rue, it was reputed to have had the power to summon the dead. Rilke's reference to "the clearest connection" here suggests the relation of the living and the dead; Rilke also mentioned this "connection" or "relation" (*Bezug*) in II.13 and in the early part of the Ninth Elegy.

I.8 Herter Norton points to a letter Rilke wrote from Toledo on November 17, 1912, in which he suggested that "one may only use the strings of lament to the full if one is determined later to play, upon them, with their means, the whole jubilance that grows and gathers behind everything burdensome, painful and endured, and without which the voices are not complete." See Rainer Maria Rilke, *Sonnets to Orpheus*, trans. by M. D. Herter Norton (New York: W. W. Norton, 1942), 143. Rilke carries this theme over into the following sonnet (I.9); for him, lament and praise were inextricably bound, not in some causal sense but because each reflected a dimension of and response to what he called "the Whole."

I.9 This sonnet voices Rilke's conviction of the union of life and death, lament and praise; the "*Doppelbereich*," which is here rendered as "double-realm," expresses this "oned oneness," as he once described it; see xiv–xv, 136–7

I.10 *The second stanza refers to the graves from the famous old cemetery of the Alyscamps, near Arles (France), which is also mentioned in [my novel],* The Notebooks of Malte Laurids Brigge.

Roman sarcophagi from Antiquity were often recommissioned in Italy and elsewhere to serve as water troughs, something Rilke noticed during his early stays in Rome. He wrote a poem about them, including it in the *New Poems*; for an English rendition of this poem, see Rainer Maria Rilke, *New Poems. A Revised Bilingual Edition*, comp. and trans. by Edward Snow (New York: Northpoint Press, 2001), 74–75. The sonnet, in pointing to this repurposing, intimates Rilke's notion of how something associated with death—a sarcophagus—could generate through the flow of water "a meandering song." Rilke's metaphor here opens this insight in ways that a prosaic description would be hard-pressed to accomplish.

I.11 Among the constellations as named in European cultures is one called Pegasus and another—that includes two of the brightest stars from the Big Dipper, Mizar and Alcor—known as the Horse and Rider. Here, however, Rilke is suggesting that the Rider might well be considered as a constellation of its own, and our "believing" in this figure might bring a delight that "suffices." Rilke also mentions the Rider as a constellation among "the stars of the land of pain" in the Tenth Elegy.

I.12   This sonnet expresses Rilke's conviction that the "symbolic" world is real, reflected in what is "here and now" (*das Hiesige*) in ways that awaken us to the connectedness, the "oneness" (*Einssein*), by which we come to know that we, in what we sense as "piecework and part" (I.16), always belong to "the Whole" (*das Ganze*).

I.13 – I.15

These sonnets belong together, each inviting a celebration of bodily experience—with all its sensuous delights. Here as often in Rilke's writings children stand as those who know this best—until the adults "turn them" around. See the Eighth Elegy: "for we already turn / the young child around so that it looks / backwards at things."

I.16   *This sonnet is addressed to a dog. The phrase "my master's hand" portrays the relationship to Orpheus, who here represents the poet's "master." The poet wants to direct this hand so that it might bless this dog for its unceasing interest and devotion, for the dog in a manner quite similar to Esau (that is, Jacob; see Genesis 27), took up its fleece for the sake of the heart of one to whom the inheritance did not come: in order to be able to participate, out of necessity and good fortune, in all humankind.*

See the discussion of Rilke's deep connection with dogs in the note to this sonnet in Herter Norton, *Sonnets*, 147–49. Rilke's own understanding of the addressee of the poem—that is, a dog—clarifies his reference to "point[ing] fingers at a smell."

I.17   It is useful to set this poem in conversation with the opening sonnet in the cycle, which Rilke begins with an image of a tree that "climbed" or "soared" or—as I have rendered the verb *steigen*—"arose" (*Da stieg ein Baum*), and then exclaims, "*O reine Übersteigung!*" That is, the call that we "climb . . . climb" mirrors what Rilke senses in Orpheus' singing, which we experience in our hearing as something as expansive as a "tall tree in the ear." To return to this sonnet, we see an image of one who climbs a tree to the point that it bends over and "arcs" as if bending itself into a lyre.

I.18   Rilke's aversion to machines is well known, though he by no means scorned technology; rather, he knew that it was a "neutral" realm, unable to distinguish value or guide how it might be utilized. He warns of this in his letter to Witold von Hulewicz; see *Selected Letters of Rainer Maria Rilke: 1902–1926*, trans. by R. F. C. Hull (London: Macmillan, 1946), 394–95.

I.20   Much has been written about this sonnet which alludes to an experience Rilke had in May, 1900, during his second trip in Russia with Lou Andreas-Salomé.

He wrote to her again in May, 1922—several months after completing the Sonnets: "And imagine one thing more, in another connection. . .I wrote, made, the horse, you know, the free happy white horse with a hobble on his foot, who once toward evening on a Volga meadow came bounding in our direction at a gallop— how I made him as an *'ex voto'* for Orpheus!—What is time?—When is the present? Across so many years he sprang, with his complete happiness, into my wide-open feeling."; cited in Herter Norton, *Sonnets*, 149.

I.21 *This little springtime song appears to me to be an "interpretation" of a peculiar dance-music I once heard children singing during the morning mass at a school in the monastery of a small convent-church in Ronda (in southern Spain). The children, keeping a steady dance-beat, sang a song unfamiliar to me, accompanied by triangle and tambourine.*

This note and the one to II.22 were the only two published in the first Insel edition of 1923; the others, attributed to Rilke, were his but not included at the urging of his publisher, Anton Kippenberg. Rilke replaced the sonnet he had first written for this place in the cycle with this one, naming it the "Child's-spring-song." After completing this poem, a copy of which he had immediately sent to Gertrud Ouckama Knoop (the mother of the deceased dancer Vera), he wrote to her again, asking her to replace the original poem with this one: "This little song here, as it came to me today when I awoke, quite finished up to the eighth line, the rest following immediately, seems to me like an interpretation of a 'Mass'—a real Mass, gaily accompanied as with hanging garlands of music; the convent children sang it to I know now what text, but in this dance-step, in the little convent church at Ronda (in southern Spain—), sang it, one can hear, to tambourine and triangle!—It fits, doesn't it, if one so wishes, into those continuities of the Sonnets to Orpheus: as the brightest spring-tone in them? (I believe so.)." Cited in Herter Norton, *Sonnets*, 150–51.

I.22 This poem, of course, refers to inventions of mechanized forms of transportation—cars and planes—that were new in Rilke's day.

I.25 Rilke addressed this poem directly to Vera Ouckama Knoop, the dancer he had met in Munich; according to a comment her mother Gertrud shared with Rilke, her last words at the edge of death were: "Now I shall dance!" For a discussion of his relationship to her, and her role in the *Sonnets*, see 139–41.

I.26 This poem tells the story of Orpheus' death, drawing on Aeschylus' account, which depicted his end as at the hand of the Maenads, urged by Dionysius to tear him to pieces in a Bacchic orgy because Orpheus preferred the worship of the rival god Apollo. What is striking here is that Orpheus' death does not end his song; even though he is "lost" in death, his song remains an "unending trace" of him: his voice lingered on in the things of nature that he had enchanted with his singing—"in lions and rocks, / in the trees and among the birds. You're singing there even now."

II.2 – 3

Mirrors play a significant role in Rilke's imagery in these sonnets, as in the Second Elegy; see also his poem to "Narzissus," in an unpublished draft of April, 1913, in Rilke, *Sämtliche Werke*, vol. 3 [*Werkausgabe*], 393; the reference to a "sixteen-pointer," referring to a buck with sixteen "points" or antlers, Rilke relates to city streetlights—which at this time were referred to as *Lüster*, or "candelabra." Here, Rilke is intent on mixing metaphors to suggest how the light of a streetlight "penetrates" or "passes through [our] impenetrability." The reference to Narcissus here is to the well-known story of the hunter from Greek mythology who was renowned for his beauty and fell in love with his own reflection in a mirroring pool of water. This is what Rilke alludes to with his reference to "the clear, relaxed [reflection of] Narzissus" in the pool.

II.4 *The unicorn has an old meaning, continually celebrated in medieval times, referring to virginity; by this is meant that this—which is nonexistent for the profane—is, as soon as it appears, in the "silvered mirror" that the virgin holds up (for example, in the tapestries of the fifteenth century) and "in her" as in a second, equally pure, equally mysterious, mirror.*

Rilke expanded on this theme in his single novel; for the full passage in an English translation, see Rainer Maria Rilke, *The Notebooks of Malte Laurids Brigge*, trans. by Stephen Mitchell (New York: Vintage Books, 1990), 127–30. Near the end of this passage Rilke wrote: "But here is still another festival; no one is invited to it. Expectation plays no role in it. Everything is here. Everything forever. The lion looks around almost menacingly: no one is allowed to come. We have never before seen her tired; is she tired? Or has she only sat down because she is holding something heavy? A monstrance, you might think. But she bends her other arm toward the unicorn, and the animal rears up, flattered, and rises and leans onto her lap. What she is holding is a mirror. Do you see: she is showing the unicorn its image—." See Rilke, *Malte Laurids Brigge*, trans. Mitchell, 130.

II.5 In a letter to Lou Andreas-Salomé, Rilke observed that "I am like the little anemone I once saw in a garden in Rome, which had opened so far during the day that it could no longer close at night! It was dreadful to see it in the dark meadow, wide open, how it still absorbed into its seemingly frantically torn-open calyx, with so much, too much, night above it, and would not be done. And beside it all its clever little sisters, each gone shut through its little measure of abundance. I too am turned so helplessly outward, hence distraught too by everything, refusing nothing, my senses overflowing, without asking me, with every disturbance; if there is a noise, I give myself up and am that noise, and since everything once adjusted to stimulation wants to be stimulated, so at bottom I want to be disturbed and am so without end. . .[which explains] why all kindness of people and of nature remains wasted on me." See Herter Norton, *Sonnets*, 155–56.

II.6   *The ancient rose was a simple "Eglantine," red and yellow, the colors that appear in flames. It blossoms in some of the gardens here in the Valais.*

See also the note to I.5 above.

II.8   *In the fourth line: the lamb (in paintings) that is only able to speak by means of a painted banner.*

One must imagine here a technique, common in medieval art, by which angels in particular "spoke" through words inscribed in scrolls, connecting them to the one they address—as is familiar, for example, in medieval paintings of the Annunciation.

The dedication in this sonnet is to Rilke's cousin who died in childhood; Rilke commemorated him in the Fourth Elegy as in several passages in *The Notebooks of Malte Laurids Brigge*. In a letter of January 24, 1924, he wrote that "I think of [Egon] often and keep returning to that figure of him which has remained indescribably moving to me. Much 'childhood', that which is sad and helpless in being a child, is embodied for me in his form, in the ruff he wore, his little neck, his chin, his beautiful brown eyes disfigured by a squint. So I evoked him once more in connection with the eighth sonnet which expresses transience. . .". Cited in Carl Sieber, *René Rilke: Die Jugend Rainer Maria Rilkes* (Hamburg: Severus Verlag, 2016), 59, and in Herter Norton, *Sonnets*, 156–57.

II.11   *With reference to the manner—in accordance with old hunting practices in certain regions characterized by "karst" topography—in which one carefully hangs scarves and waves them in a particular way so that the peculiarly pale grotto-doves who live there are chased forth from their subterranean repose in order to capture them when, startled, they fly out.*

Rilke became familiar with this topography, which he had explored in the area inland of Trieste, a region well-known for its limestone "karst" caves, during his long stay at Duino Castle in the late Fall of 1911 and the Winter/ Spring of 1912.

II.12   Daphne's father, the river-god Peneus, transformed his daughter into a laurel tree to avoid her being captured by Apollo; for this reason, the tree later became sacred to and revered by Apollo. The transformed Daphne, in turn, "addresses" us through Rilke's words here, inviting us to transform ourselves into wind. Note the allusion to the laurel (tree) in the opening lines of Rilke's Ninth Elegy.

II.13 This was the single poem Rilke transcribed and sent to Gertrud Knoop, Vera's mother, when he wrote to her to tell her of the "completion" of the sonnets after the second set of twenty-nine had "arrived" in that auspicious month of February, 1922. Note also Rilke's reiteration of this theme in the closing lines of the Eighth Elegy:

> Who, then, has turned us around so that,
>
> whatever we do, we have the posture
>
> of one departing? Like one standing
>
> on the last hill that shows him his valley
>
> again in its entirety, who turns, pauses, lingers –,
>
> thus we live, always taking our leave.

II.18 The poem addresses one simply called "Tänzerin," the feminine form of "dancer"; this refers to Vera Knoop as the poem tells of how she "transposed" loss—"all that is passing into motion"—in this case through the creative expression of music and writing; see 139–41.

II.19 This sonnet recalls the horror Rilke felt during his first stay in Paris in 1902, living as he did near the Parisian hospital named Hôtel-Dieu. He daily witnessed the suffering and agony of those who came hoping for help—often arriving early in the morning and remaining outside until they could receive medical attention. He recounts this experience, and his revulsion to it, in the opening lines of *The Notebooks of Malte Laurids Brigge*: "So this is where people come to live, though it seemed to me that they came to die here. I was there. I saw: hospitals. I saw a person who stumbled and collapsed. People gathered around him and I was spared the rest..." (my translation).

II.21 Rilke had long hoped to visit Persia (Iran), inspired by stories shared with him by Lou Andreas-Salomé's husband, Friedrich Carl Andreas, an historian of Persian culture, who had done extensive field work in southern Iran. Andreas eventually held the chair for western Asiatic philology at the University of Göttingen (from 1903 until his death in 1930). Thus, Rilke could only "sing" the celebrated gardens—which he did not "know" experientially—that he longed to see, those "incomparable" ones found in the ancient Persian cities of Isfahan and Shiraz, by imagining them as he does in this sonnet. The reference to gardens "poured into glass" recalls the fascination he felt, during his first trip to Italy with his mother, with the Murano glass-art of Venice. The final images referring to Persian carpets call to mind those that were hung on the walls in

Muzot as tapestries; this was common in ancient stone buildings as a means of preserving the heat and minimizing the penetration of moisture.

II.22 The bell mentioned in the second stanza probably refers to the great iron bell in the Kremlin tower built by Boris Godunov ca. 1600, which he heard ringing out during the Easter Vigil on Holy Saturday (night) in Moscow, during his first visit to Russia in 1899. He later wrote that "I have experienced Easter [in my life] but a single time: it was that long, unfamiliar, peculiar, and thrilling night when all the [Russian] people pressed upon [Lou and me], and the great bell called by the name 'Iwan Welikij' pounded upon me in the darkness, blow upon blow. This was my Easter, and I believe it will suffice for the rest of my life." I cite this letter and discuss the decisive significance of Rilke's experiences in Russia in the Afterword to *Prayers of a Young Poet* (Brewster, MA: Paraclete Press, 2016), 99–101. The reference to Karnak recalls his trip to Egypt, another shaping experience in his life that he later described as exceeding language: "One cannot take it in," he wrote to his wife Clara on January 18, 1911, going on to say that "This inconceivable temple-world of Karnak, at which on the very first evening, and again yesterday, in the moon just starting to wane, I gazed, gazed, gazed,—my God, one gathers oneself together, looks with all one's powers of belief through both totally focused eyes—and yet it begins beyond them, stretches everywhere far beyond them (only a god can command such a field of view)—and there stands a lotus-bud column, solitary, surviving, and one cannot grasp it, so purely does it stand there, out beyond one's life." Cited by Snow, *Sonnets*, 122.

II.23 *Dedicated to the reader.*

II.25 *This is the counterpart to the springtime song of children from the First Part of Sonnets (I.21).*

II.28 *Dedicated to Vera Ouckama Knoop.*

As mentioned in the Afterword (see 139–41), Rilke links this poem addressed directly to Vera to Orpheus who "comes and goes" (see I.5).

II.29 *Dedicated to one of Vera's friends.*

ENDNOTES

1   From von Hoffmannsthal's letter of May 25, 1923; in *Hugo von Hofmannsthal and Rainer Maria Rilke. Briefwechsel: 1899–1925*, ed. by Rudolf Hirsch and Ingeborg Schnack (Frankfurt am Main: Insel Verlag, 1978), 835; also cited in Rainer Maria Rilke, *Werke. Kommentierte Ausgabe in vier Bänden*, vol. 2, *Gedichte 1910–1926*, ed. by Manfred Engel and Ulrich Fülleborn (Frankfurt am Main and Leipzig: Insel Verlag, 1996), 712. This is the four-volume critical edition known as the "Kommentierte Ausgabe"; it is cited here as "KA" followed by the volume number and pagination. All translations included in the notes for this volume are my own unless otherwise cited.

2   From Rilke's letter to Witold von Hulewicz, November 13, 1925, in Rainer Maria Rilke, *Briefe aus Muzot 1921 bis 1926* (Leipzig: Insel Verlag, 1935), 338. All further references to this collection are noted as *"Briefe"* with the volume and pagination noted. The portion of this letter cited here is also found in KA II, 711.

3   This excerpt is from Rilke's letter to his mother dated July 28, 1921; Ingeborg Schnack, editor, *Rainer Maria Rilke. Chronik seines Lebens und seines Werkes 1875–1926*, erweiterte Neuausgabe, ed. by Renate Scharffenberg (Frankfurt am Main and Leipzig: Insel Verlag, 1975), 737.

4   From Rilke's letter to Gräfin Sizzo, April 12, 1923; in KA II, 708.

5   From Rilke's letter to his publisher, Katharina Kippenberg, February 23, 1922; in KA II, 708.

6   From Rilke's letter to Xaver von Moos, April 20, 1923; in KA II, 710.

7   From Rilke's letter to Gudi Nölke, April 23, 1923; in KA II, 710.

8   From Rilke's letter to Nanny von Escher, December 22, 1923; in KA II, 599.

9   From an untitled and, during his lifetime, unpublished poem that begins with these lines; in KA II, 276.

10   Ann Wroe, *Orpheus. The Song of Life* (London: Jonathan Cape, 2011), 4. Rilke

had received a copy of Ovid's *Metamorphoses*, in a French translation, from his lover at the time, Balladine Klossowska, whom he affectionately called "Merline." She also gave him a postcard bearing an engraving of Orpheus by the Renaissance Italian artist Cima de Conegliano (ca. 1459–ca. 1517); Rilke placed this image above his writing desk.

11 The phrase is from one of Rilke's early poems, included in the *Book of Hours*: "Let everything happen to you: beauty and terror." See Rainer Maria Rilke, *Prayers of a Young Poet*, trans. by Mark S. Burrows, 3rd rev. ed. (Brewster, MA: Paraclete Press, 2024; previous editions: Paraclete Press, 2012 and 2nd rev. ed. 2015), 70.

12 All references to the *Sonnets to Orpheus*, in the Introduction and Afterword, refer to them (as here) by identifying the First or Second Part and number (e.g., II.16 refers to the sixteenth sonnet from the Second Part). I discuss this theme, which is central in the *Sonnets* and in those of the *Elegies* Rilke composed in Muzot (including the Eighth and Ninth, included in this volume); see viii, 131–32.

13 From Rilke's letter to Nanny von Escher, December 22, 1923; in KA II, 599.

14 From Rilke's letter to Witold von Hulewicz, November 13, 1925; see *Briefe* II, 480, 481.

15 *Briefe* II, 480.

16 From Rilke's letter of December 22, 1923, to Nanny von Escher; in *Briefe* II, 431.

17 Lines like these suggest what Martin Heidegger—inspired by Rilke—called "meditative reflection," a pondering that exhilarates us with that sense of inner spaciousness. Heidegger spoke of this as "*das besinnliche Nachdenken*" in contrast to "*das rechnende Denken*." He discusses this in an essay of 1959, published under the title Gelassenheit (Pfullingen, Germany: Verlag Günther Neske, 1959), 14–15. An English translation of this treatise was published as Martin Heidegger, "Memorial Address," and included in *Discourse on Thinking*, trans. by John M. Anderson and E. Hans Freund (New York: Harper Colophon Books, 1966). Only the former, "meditative reflection," can grant us, Heidegger argued, "the possibility of dwelling in the world in a totally different way" (Heidegger, *Discourse on Thinking*, 55). Heidegger expands on this point in an essay written on the twenty-fifth anniversary of Rilke's death entitled "Wozu Dichter?"; this essay, in an English translation, is entitled "What Are Poets For?" and is in Heidegger, *Poetry, Language, Thought*, trans. by Albert Hofstadter (New York: Harper and Row), 91–142. Rilke coined the word *Weltinnenraum* to speak of this; for my discussion of this—rendered as "inner spaciousness," "spacious

innerness," or simply "inner space"—see my essay "'What Deepens the Deep for Us': Poetry, Contemplation, and the Art of Reading," in *Spiritus* 23 (Fall, 2023), 269–94.

18　From Rilke's letter to Gräfin Margot Sizzo-Noris-Crouy, April 12, 1923; in Rilke, *Briefe* II, 406.

19　Rilke, *Briefe* II, 406.

20　See *Letters to Merline (1919–1922)*, trans. by Jesse Browner (New York: Paragon House, 1989), 29.

21　See also I.16, I.18, I.20.

22　See xvi – xvii, 136–39.

23　For a penetrating discussion of Rilke on this point, see William Waters, *Poetry's Touch. On Lyric Address* (Ithaca and London: Cornell University Press, 2003), 117–21.

24　Rilke's discovery of "things" was decisive for his work as a writer; this reflects Rodin's influence on him during two long periods of the poet's residence in Paris. "Things," as he came to understand them, were part of "the Whole"; their aliveness mattered for its own sake, and not because of what they might mean for us.

25　From Rilke's letter to Nanny von Escher, December 22, 1923; in *Briefe aus Muzot*, 220. Rilke went on to remark that one should "seek the plot [*Handlung*] of these poems" in terms of these themes (see above, n. 8), "and occasionally this is present, simply and powerfully, in the foreground" of the *Sonnets*. See *Briefe aus Muzot*, 220–21.

26　For a discussion of the complicated story of Rilke's composition of the *Elegies* over the period beginning in January, 1912, and continuing until their completion in February of 1922, see KA II, 605–11; for a description of his writing of the *Sonnets*, see KA II, 706–7.

27　From Rilke's letter to Gräfin Sizzo, April 12, 1923; cited in *Rainer Maria Rilke. Chronik*, 824.

28　From Rilke's letter to Witold von Hulewicz, November 13, 1925; in *Briefe* II, 485.

29　From "The Ninth Elegy," ll. 11–12.

30　From Rilke's letter to Lotte Hepner, November 8, 1915; in *Briefe* II, 52.

31　J. B. Leishman, from the Introduction to *Sonnets to Orpheus* (London: Leonard and Virginia Woolf at the Hogarth Press, 1936), 11–12.

32　These are the opening stanzas of an untitled poem that remained unpublished during Rilke's lifetime; see KA II, 156.

33　See above, n. 2.

34   *Die Aufzeichnungen des Malte Laurids Brigge* [*The Notebooks of Malte Laurids Brigge*] (Frankfurt am Main: Insel Verlag, 1951), 25. In one of the many lyric moments within this modernist "novel," Rilke goes on to describe, in a memorable passage, the peculiar origin of poems: "For the sake of a poem, one must see many cities, people, and things, one must come to know animals, one must feel how birds fly and know the gestures with which small flowers open to the morning. One must be able to reflect on paths in unknown regions, on unexpected encounters and on departures that one had long expected,— on the days of childhood that remain unexplained, on parents whom one hurt when they sought to offer some delight that one failed to grasp ... And it is not yet enough simply to have acquired memories. One must be able to forget them in their plurality and find the patience to wait until they come again. For it is not finally about memories. Only when they become blood in us, seeing and gesture, nameless and no longer distinguishable from ourselves, only then can it happen that in a rare hour the first word of a poem arises amid them and goes forth from them.'"

35   From Rilke's letter to Magda von Hattingberg, February 13, 1915; cited in *The Poet's Guide to Life. The Wisdom of Rilke*, ed. and trans. by Ulrich Baer (New York: The Modern Library, 2005), 143.

36   From Rilke's letter to his Polish translator, Witold von Hulewicz, November 25, 1925; in *Briefe aus Muzot*, 334–5. This theme emerges with a poignant if also startling directness in the writings of the Danish writer Inger Christensen; see her essay "The Seven Within the Die" in *The Condition of Secrecy*, trans. Susanna Nied (New York: New Directions Publishing Corp., 2018), 115–25.

37   From Rilke's letter to Witold von Hulewicz, November 13, 1925; in *Briefe aus Muzot*, 338.

38   Wroe, *Orpheus*, 4.

39   The reference is to the Simon and Garfunkel song of the same name, written in 1964; the opening stanza of that song accords with Rilke's sense of the important resonance of silence in our lives—an expression of the "radiant darkness" he himself sensed in the Sonnets: "Hello darkness, my old friend / I've come to talk with you again / Because a vision softly creeping / Left its seeds while I was sleeping / And the vision that was planted in my brain / Still remains / Within the sound of silence."

40   From Rilke's letter to Gräfin Margot Sizzo-Noris-Crouy, April 12, 1923; *Briefe* II, 40–9. This passage finds an illuminating discussion in Louth, *Rilke*, 459.

41   From Rilke's letter to Gertrud Ouckama Knoop, undated (ca. mid-January, 1922); in *Briefe aus Muzot*, 83–8.

42   The current US Surgeon General, Dr. Vivek Murthy, recently wrote of "the epidemic of loneliness and isolation" inflicting many in these times; see https://www.hhs.gov/about/news/2023/05/03/new-surgeon-general-advisory-raises-alarm-about-devastating-impact-epidemic-loneliness-isolation-united-states.html (accessed on July 15, 2023).

43   This reference is from a letter Rilke wrote to Gertrud Ouckama Knoop, marveling at her late daughter's capacity—in the face of a debilitating and fatal illness—to "open her heart entirely to the unity of this living and resilient world, this assent to life, this joyful, stirring sense of belonging to everything that is here, all the way to the end—alas, and surely not only to what is here?! No, (what she could not have known in the first attacks of this ending and departure!)—into the *Whole,* which is much more than what is here." *Briefe aus Muzot,* 83–4.

44   This is an untitled poem of 1921, unpublished during Rilke's lifetime; he wrote it as a dedication to Leonie Zacharias, inscribed in a copy of his novel *Malte* that he gave her; in Rilke, *Sämtliche Werke,* vol. 3, 249; for the poem's origin, see also KA 2, 588..

45   Among the wide circle of translations of these poems, I find the early version of M. D. Herter Norton (first published in 1942) to be particularly instructive (Rainer Maria Rilke, *Sonnets to Orpheus,* trans. by M. D. Herter Norton [New York: W. W. Norton, 1942]). Unlike most others, her translation stays close in the English to the "experience" of Rilke's often complex and dynamic linguistic constructions—something that is extremely difficult to do when moving from an inflected language, like German, to an uninflected one like English. She rarely simplifies Rilke's phraseology, consistently resisting the tempting possibility of smoothing out his often broken and generally abrupt syntax. As she put it in the Foreword to that edition, "[t]he translator's prime effort has gone into the translation itself, into the search for equivalents—not dictionary equivalents, but those that should take in the special flavor, the corresponding ambiguity, the poet's usage, the 'secret name,'" the last image taken from one of Rilke's letters in which he answered a correspondent's query about the *Sonnets* by insisting that "no poem in the *Sonnets to Orpheus* means anything that is not fully written out there, often, it is true, with its most secret name." See Herter Norton, *Sonnets to Orpheus,* 10–11. At the other end of the spectrum, Don Paterson's rendition is one he prefers to call a "version," entitling the book simply *Orpheus;* his poems range far from the original treasury of Rilke's metaphoric world and peculiar German diction, yet give voice to a rendition that is often as thrilling to read in English as Rilke's is in German—even if it strays far

afield from the original; see Don Paterson, *Orpheus* (London: Faber and Faber, 2007).

46   These three volumes from *Das Stunden-Buch* appeared as *Das Buch vom mönchi-schen Leben*, *Das Buch von der Pilgerschaft*, and *Das Buch von der Armut und vom Tode*, ed. Gotthard Fermor with (German) Introductions by Mark S. Burrows (Gütersloh: Gütersloher Verlagshaus, 2014, 2016, and 2018 respectively). During the process of completing and publishing these volumes, we shaped— together with the photographer Klaus Diederich, composer and pianist Josef Marschall, and saxophonist Jürgen Hiekel—three "musical-lyrical" programs based on the poems from *Das Stunden-Buch*, taking them on the road during those years in performances that took us to cities and towns across Germany.

Mark S. Burrows, M.Div., Ph.D. is an award-winning translator, poet, and historian whose work explores the intersection of poetry and spirituality, theology and the arts; his academic work explores the field of medieval history and culture with a particular focus on mysticism and monastic literature. He taught in graduate theological schools in the US for three decades before accepting a professorship at the Protestant University of Applied Sciences in Bochum, Germany, where he taught until 2020. During that period, he was an invited member of the "Bochumer Literaten," a professional writers' group that sponsored public readings and literary events in the city. His poetry appears in numerous journals and anthologies internationally, and his collection *The Chance of Home* was praised for the ways its "wise and tender poems practice 'long listening.'" He also serves as Poetry Editor for Wildhouse Publishing and for the journal Spiritus. His ground-breaking translation of Rilke's "Prayers," published as *Prayers of a Young Poet*, is the only English version of these poems, which later appeared as Part I of *The Book of Hours*. He also collaborated on a three-volume German edition of Rilke's Das Stundenbuch (2014 – 2018), in conjunction with the "Bonn Rilke Project," and "performed" these poems with that ensemble in cities and towns across Germany. His English-language translations include a volume of poems by the Iranian-German poet SAID, *99 Psalms* (2013), as well as the first English translation of poems by the Jewish-German poet Hilde Domin, *The Wandering Radiance. Selected Poems of Hilde Domin* (2023). Together with Jon M. Sweeney he has published three collections of meditative poems inspired by Meister Eckhart, including most recently *Meister Eckhart's Book of Darkness and Light* (2023). His forthcoming book, also with Monkfish Book Publishing Co., is *You Are the Future: Living the Questions with Rainer Maria Rilke*, co-authored with Stephanie Dowrick. He lives and writes in Camden, ME. www.soul-in-sight.org

Printed in the USA
CPSIA information can be obtained
at www.ICGtesting.com
JSHW081221040524
62359JS00002B/2